#cloudart

This book is dedicated to all the people in my
life who gave me pictures of clouds, and who
were forced to look at my drawings.
Thank-you 😊

This cloud started my hobby of doodling on them.
My daughter took the picture for me as we drove home from
my mom's. I pointed, she clicked.

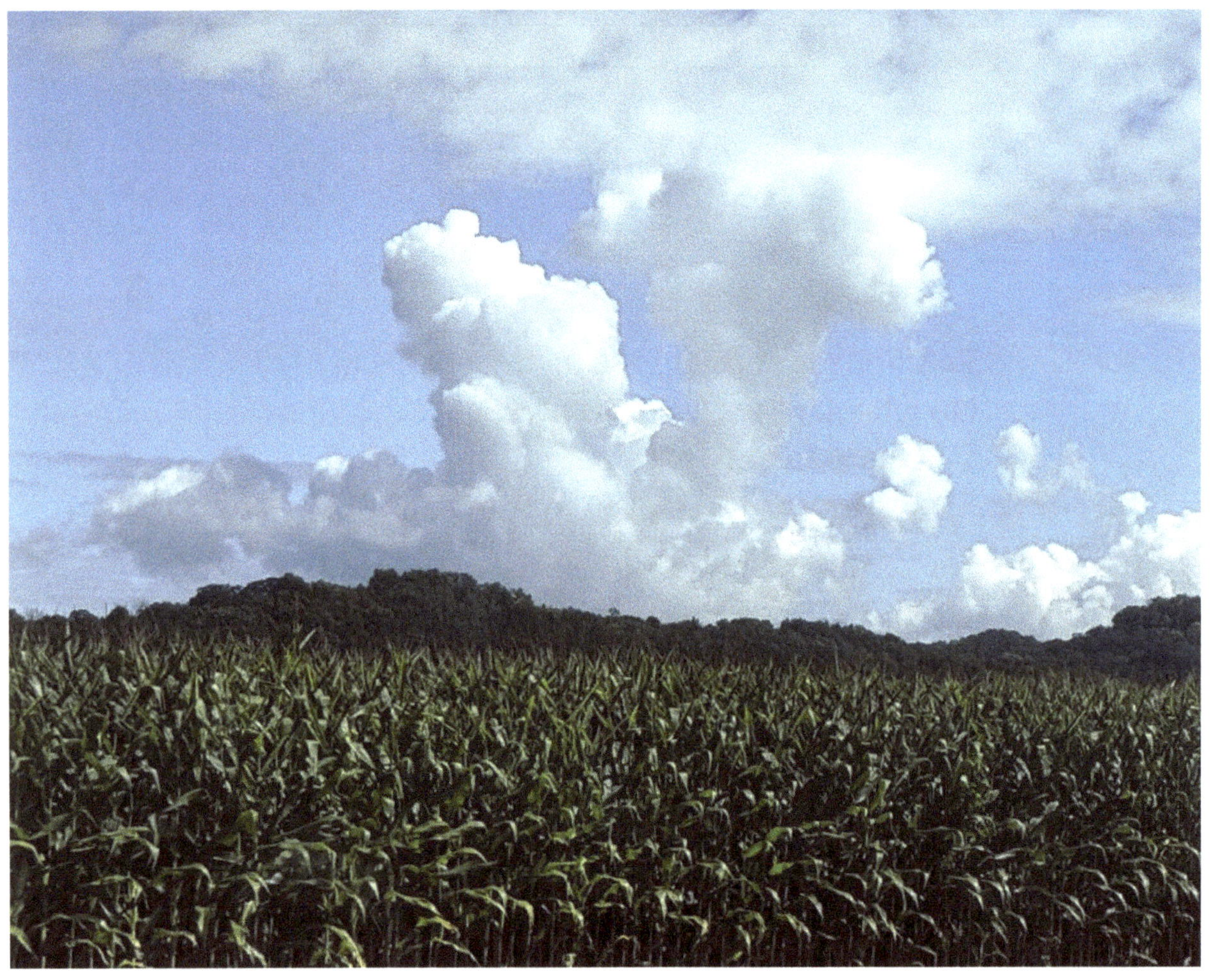

I've titled it: **Gnome Riding a Dinosaur**

I even gave him a little backpack

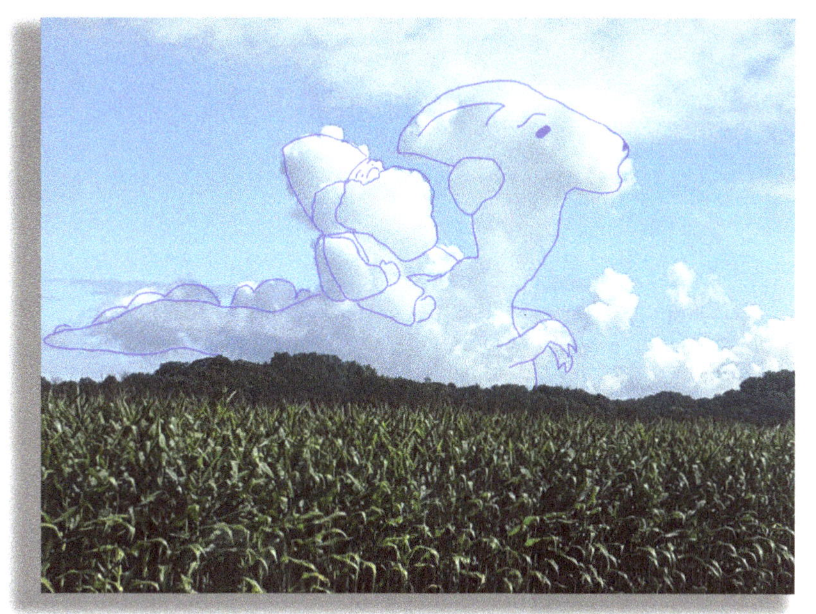

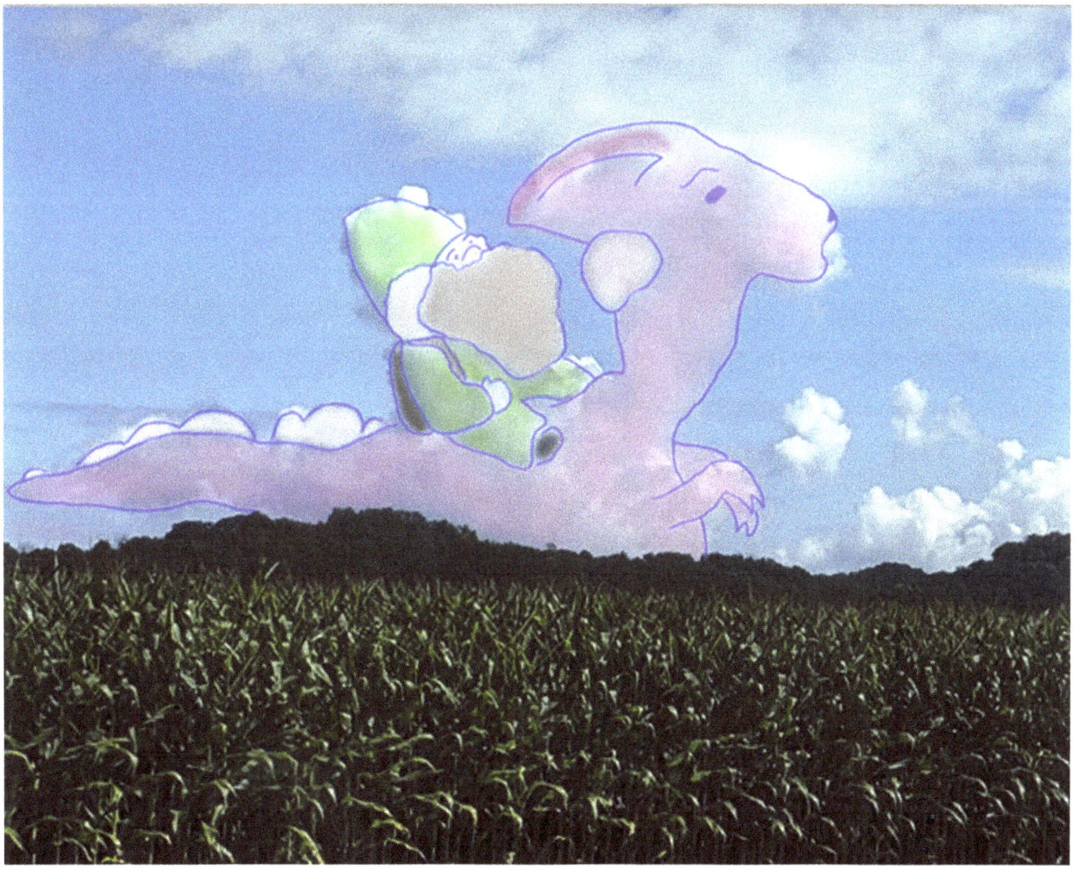

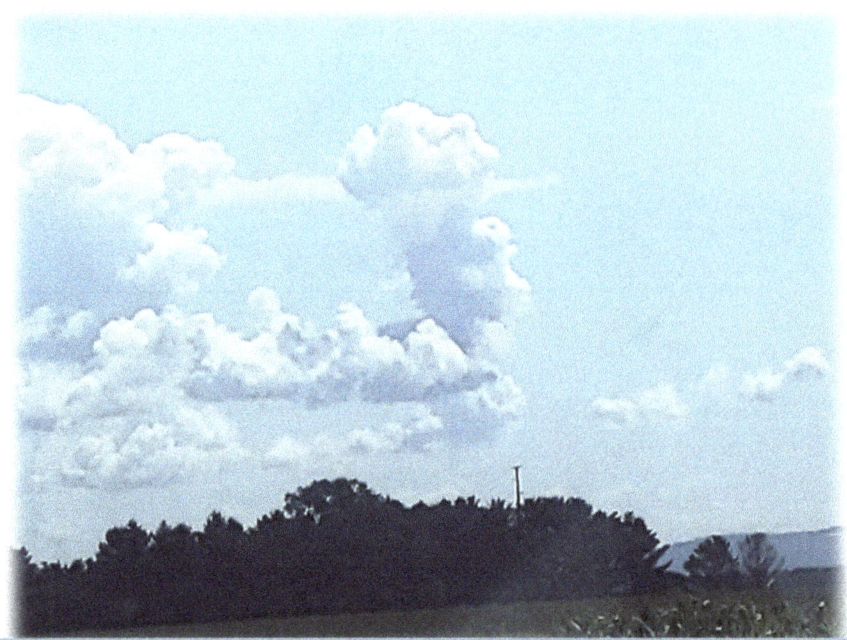

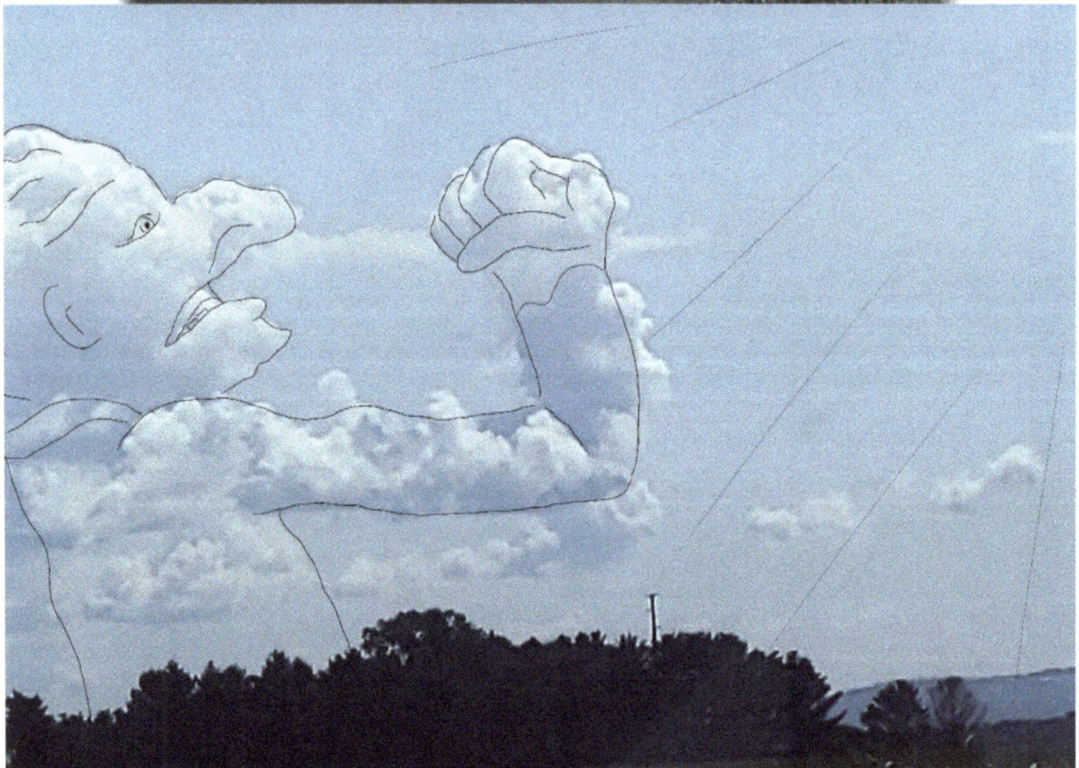

Old Man Yelling At The Sun

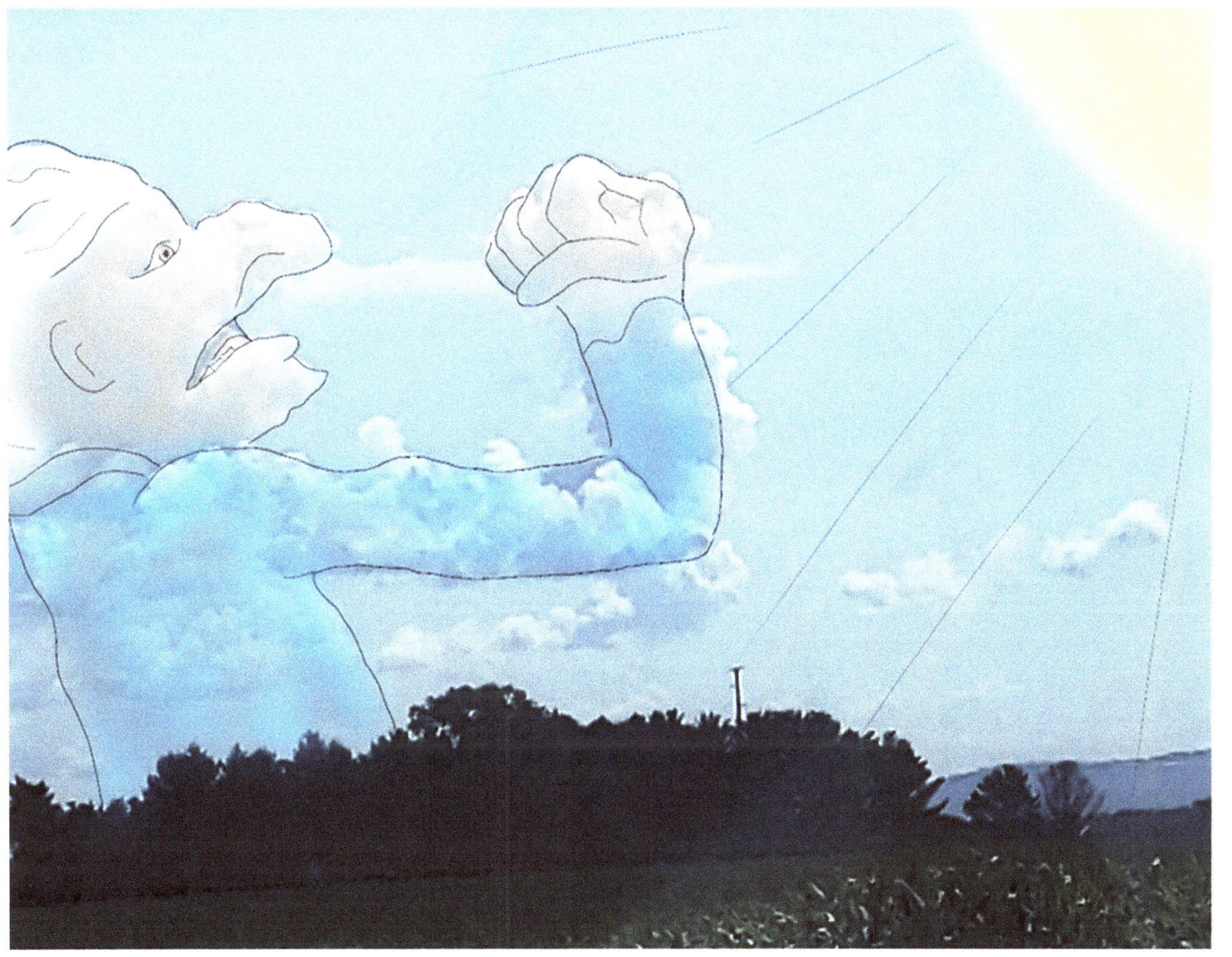

This was taken the same day as the gnome picture.
I would've liked him to have had more hair, but my daughter
thought I only wanted a picture of the "fist" portion.
It still works. ☺

I saw these two while walking during my lunch break.
They were floating above where I work.

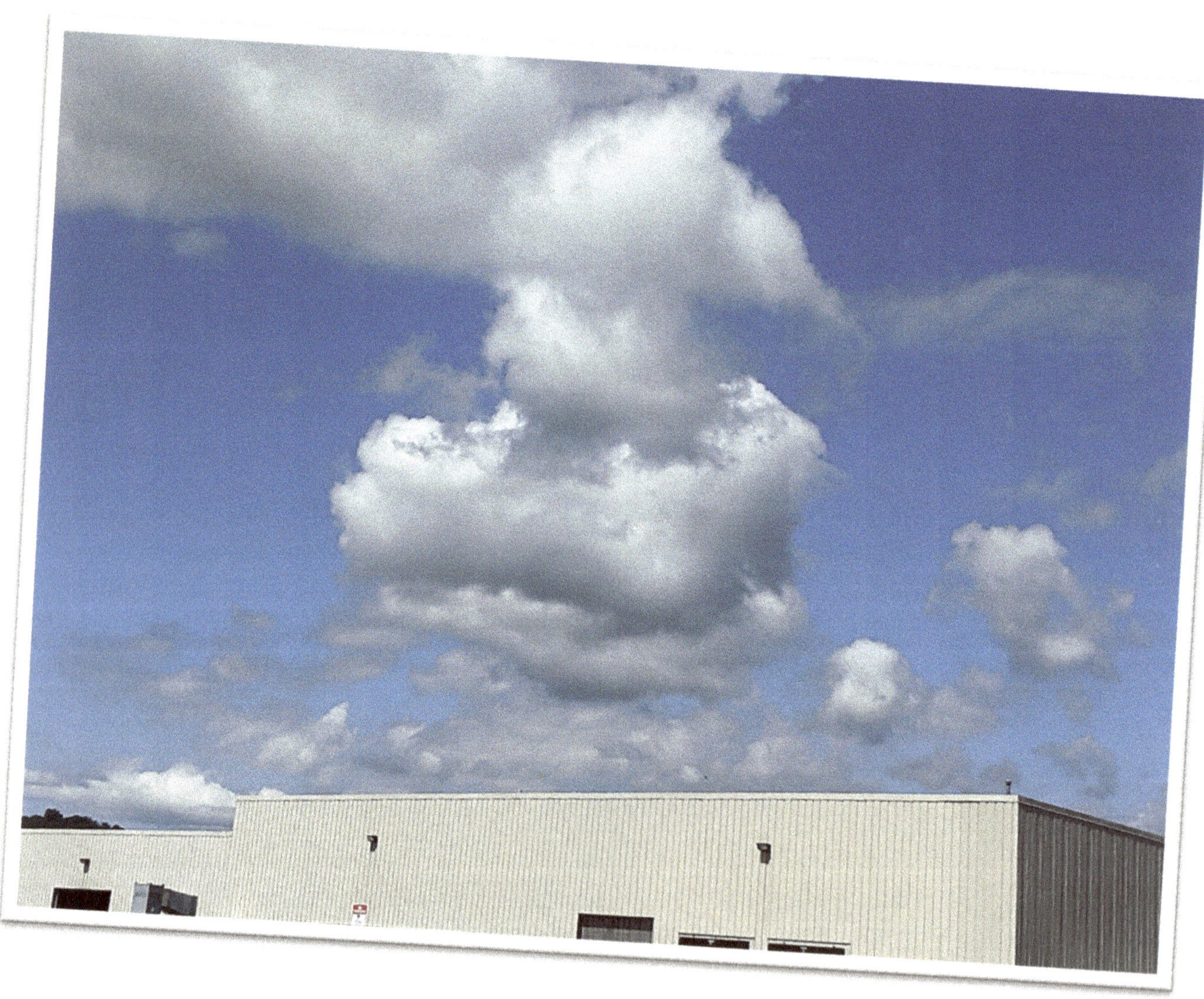

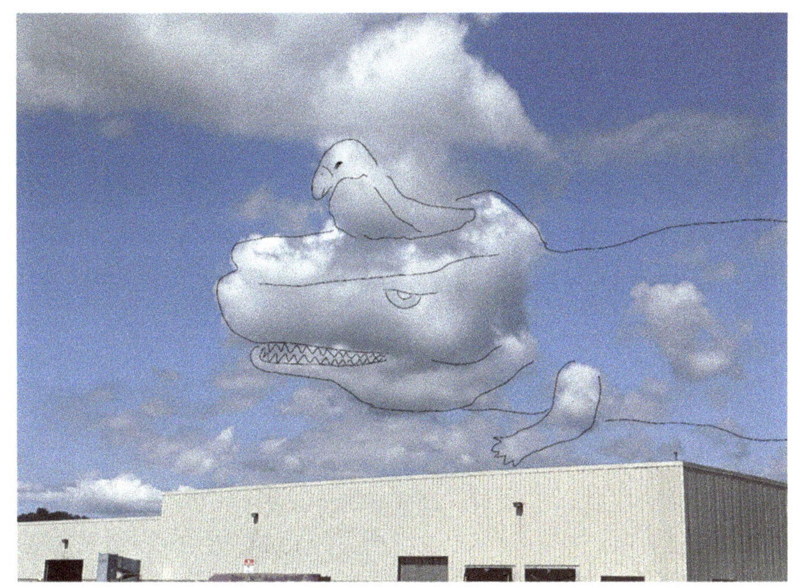

Bird on an Alligator

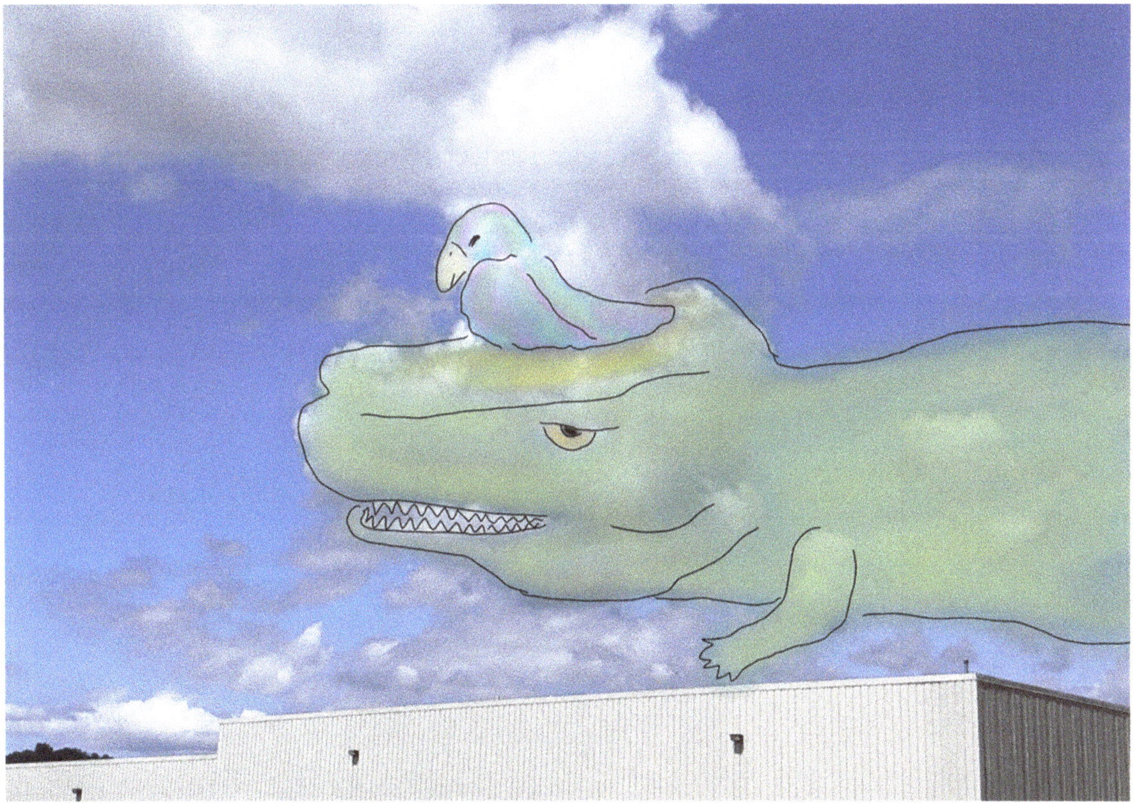

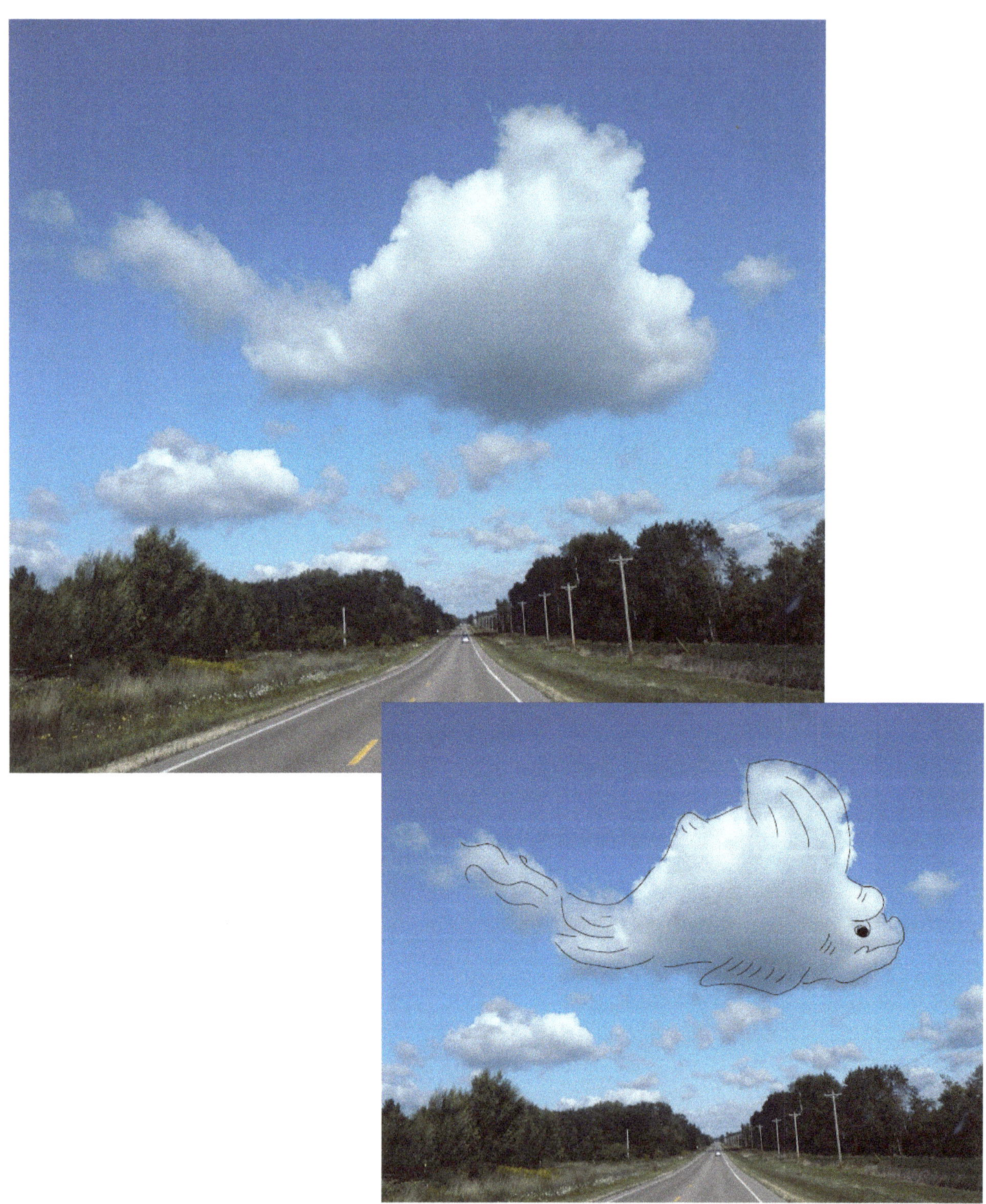

My friend sent this picture hoping I'd see the same
thing he did. I did not. He saw a turtle and I saw:

Angry Fish Kicking Up Sand

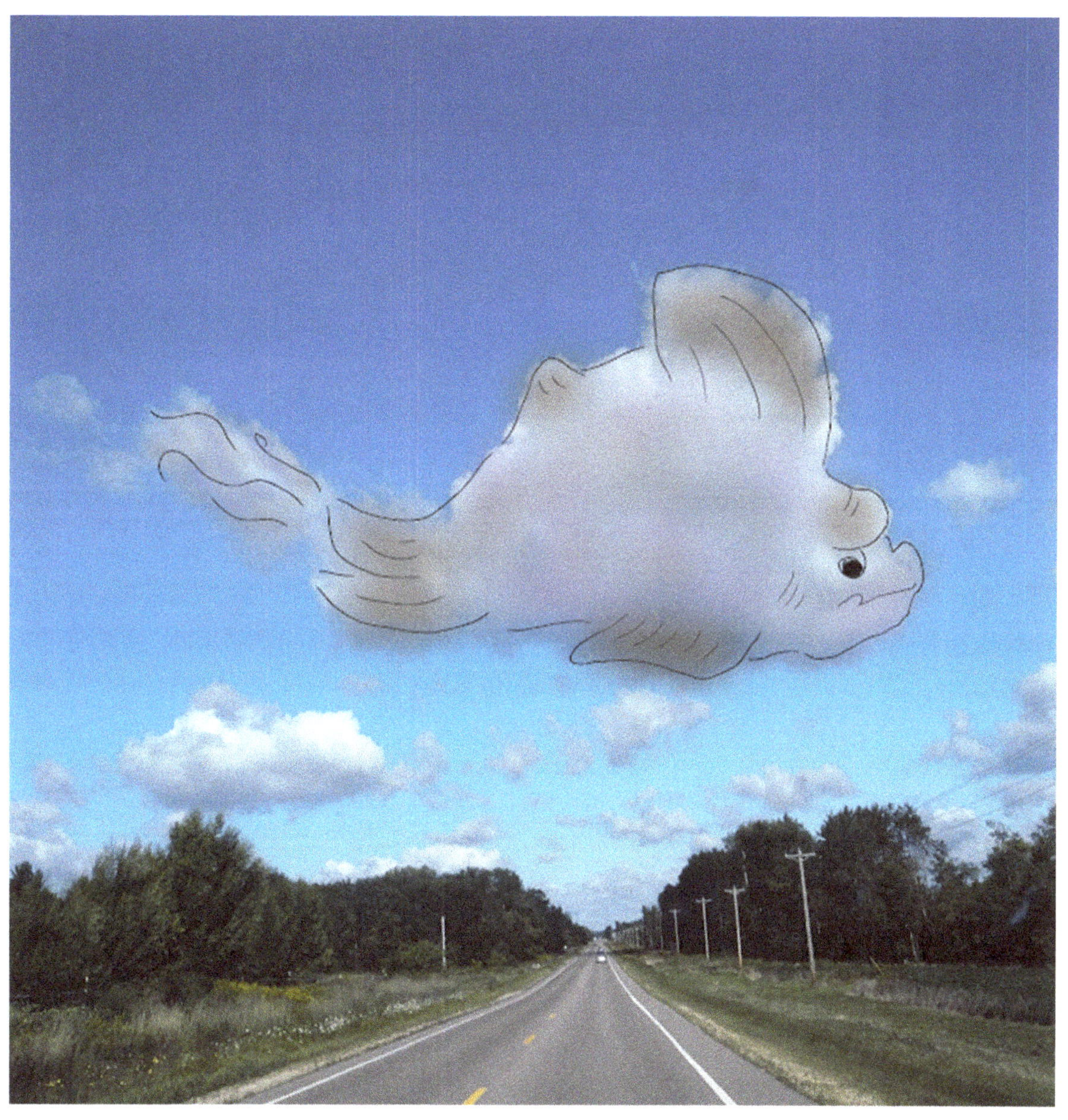

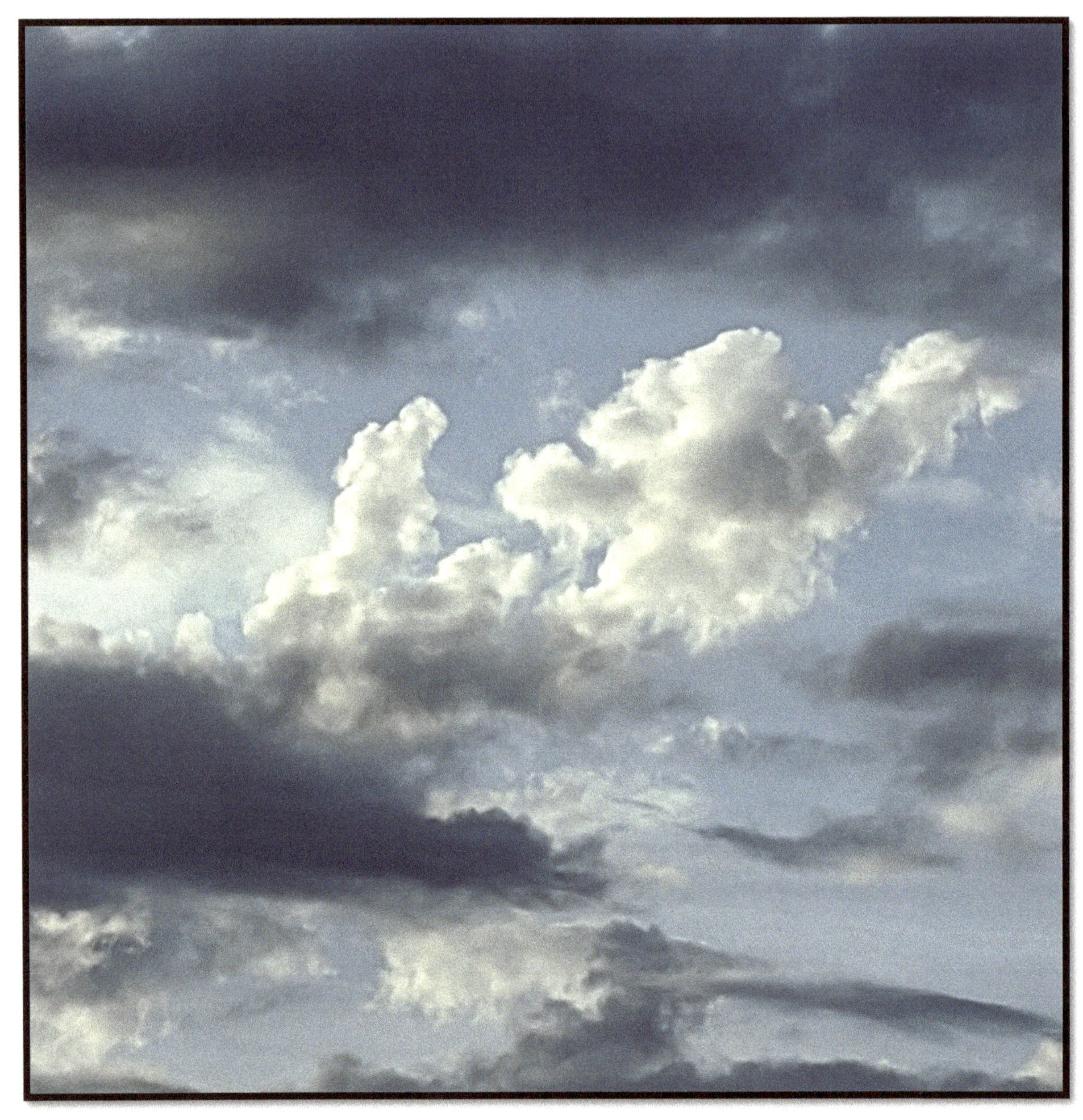

A bird? A plane? No. It's: **Woman Flying!**

(capes not required ☺)

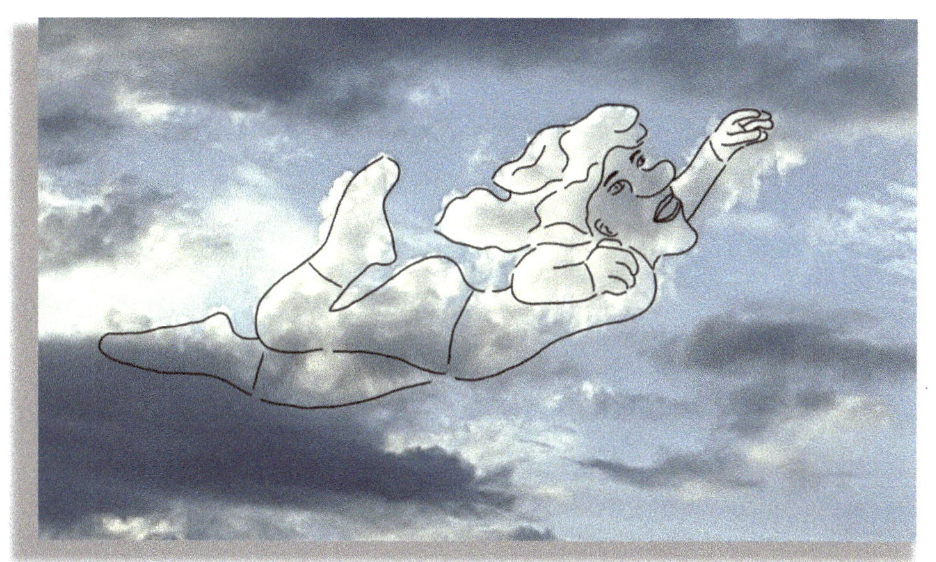

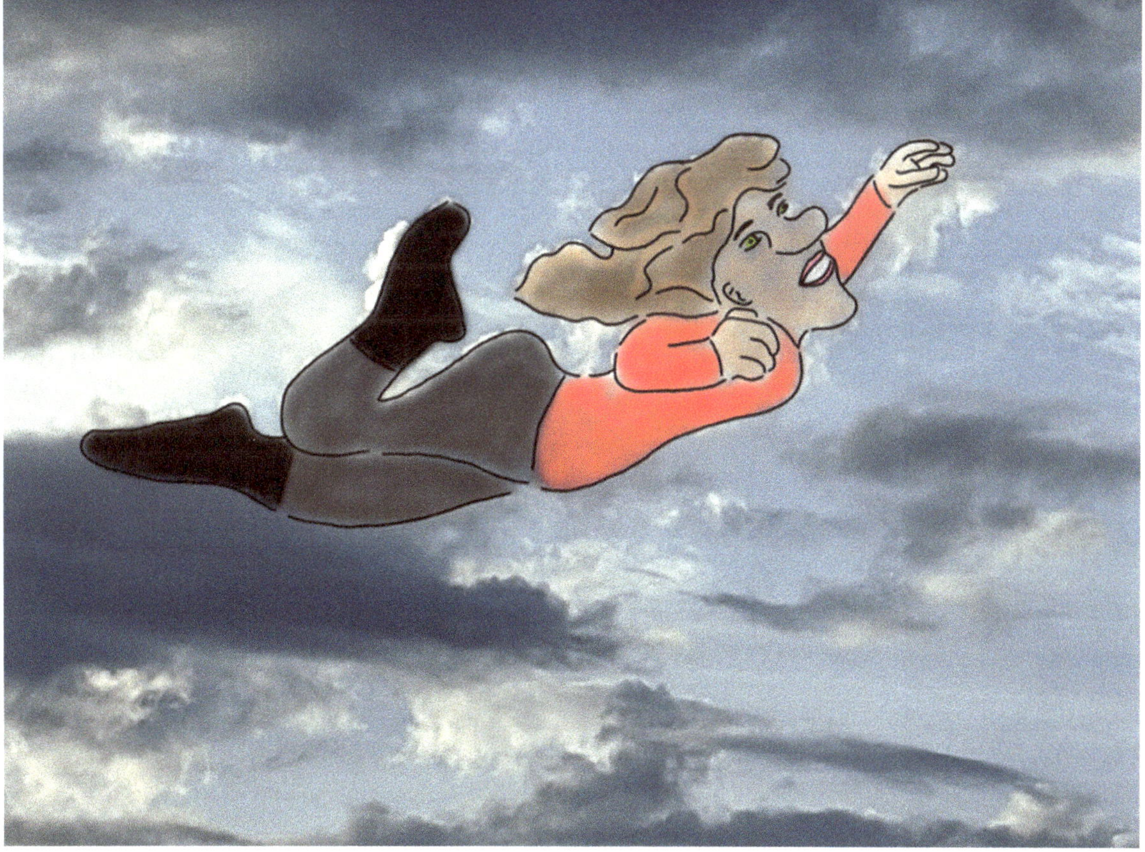

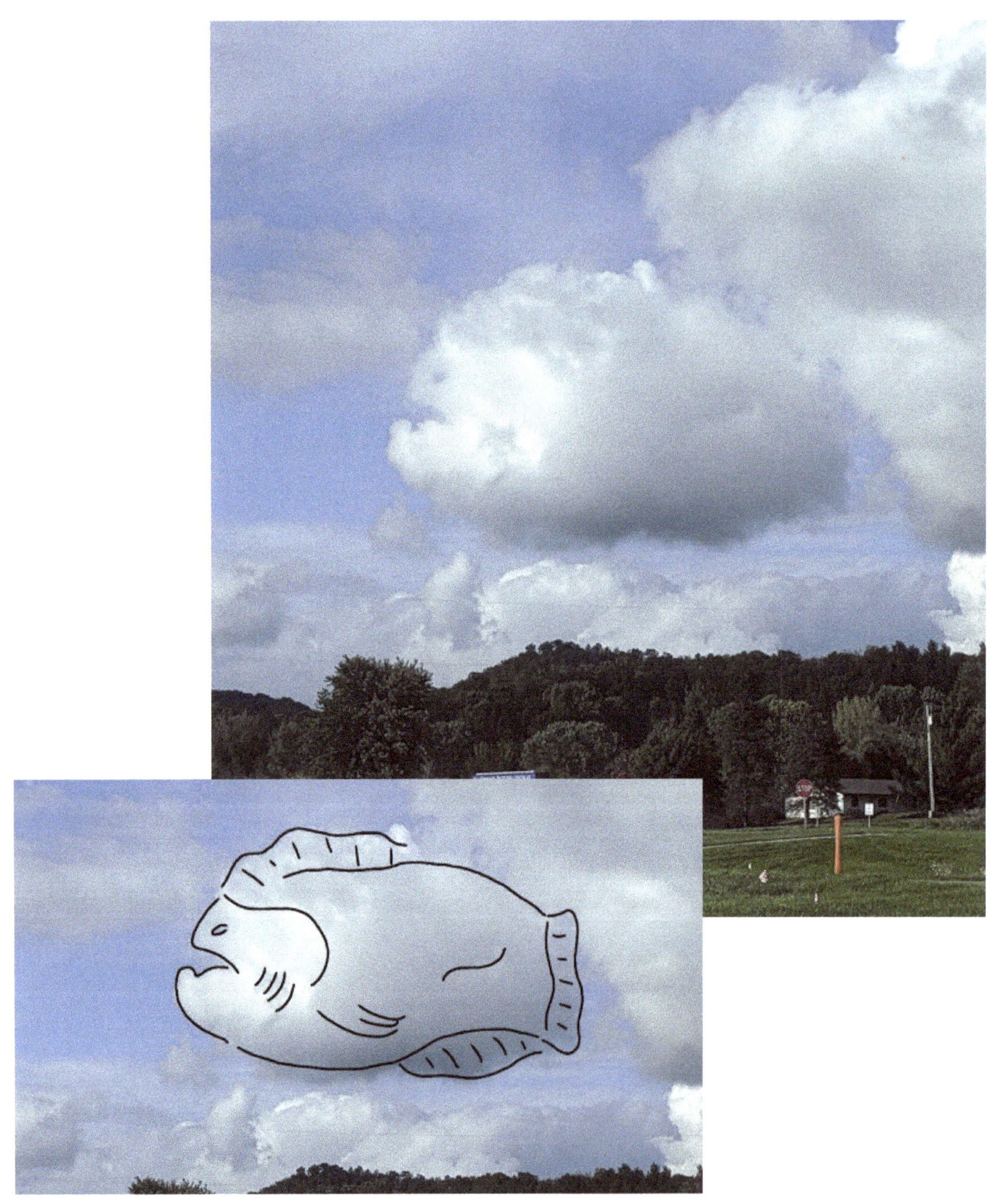

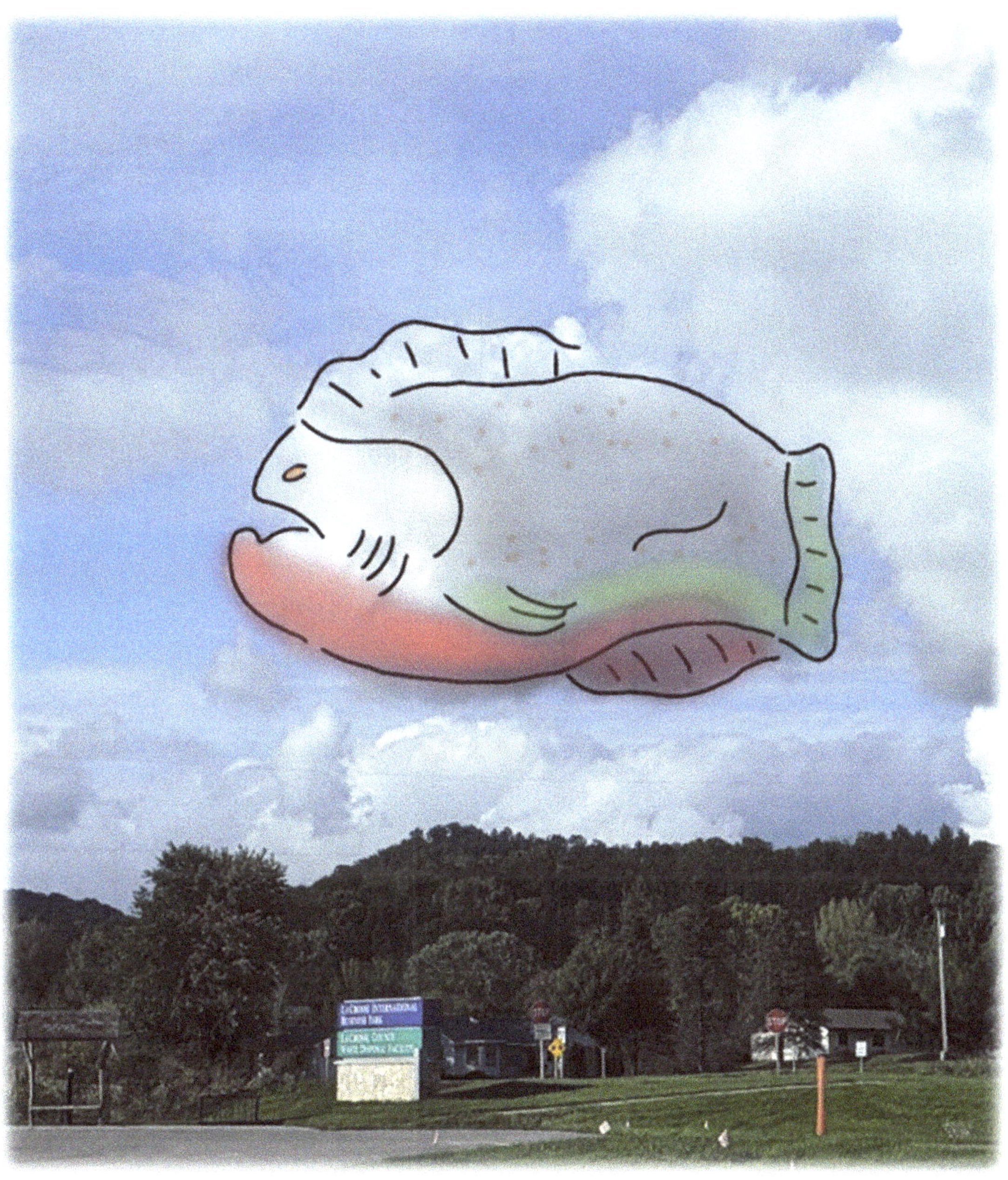

I had wanted a piranha, but my coloring
isn't right so now I have a hybrid:

Piranha/ Salmon

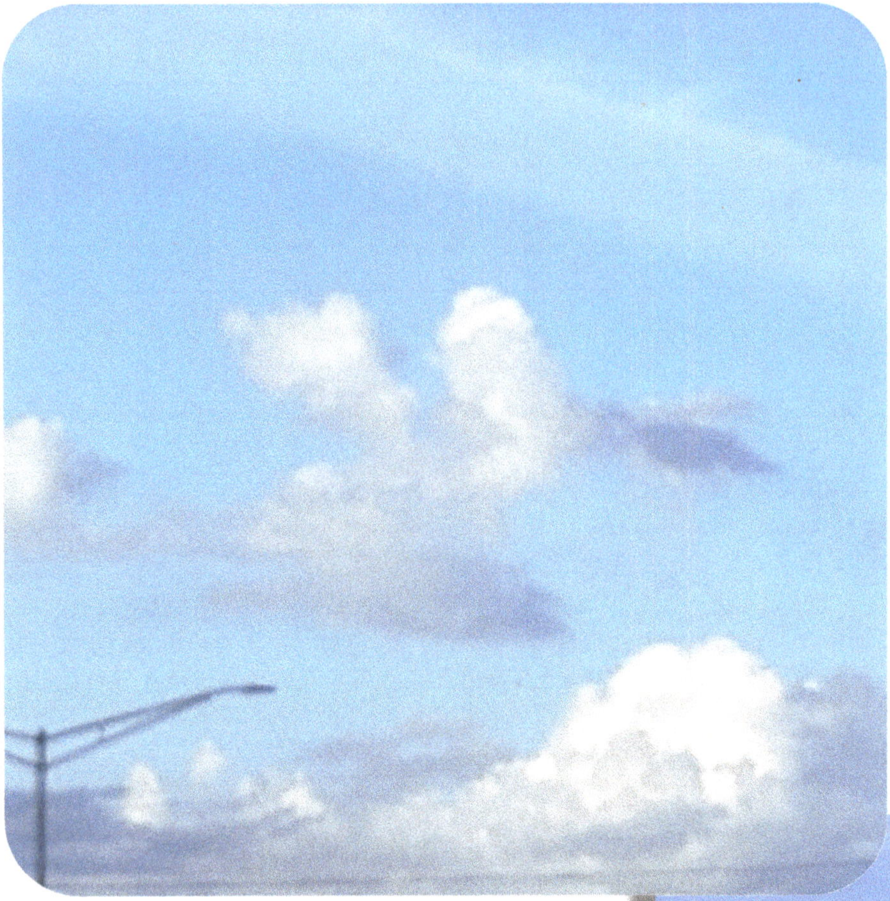

**Pelican with
a Fish**

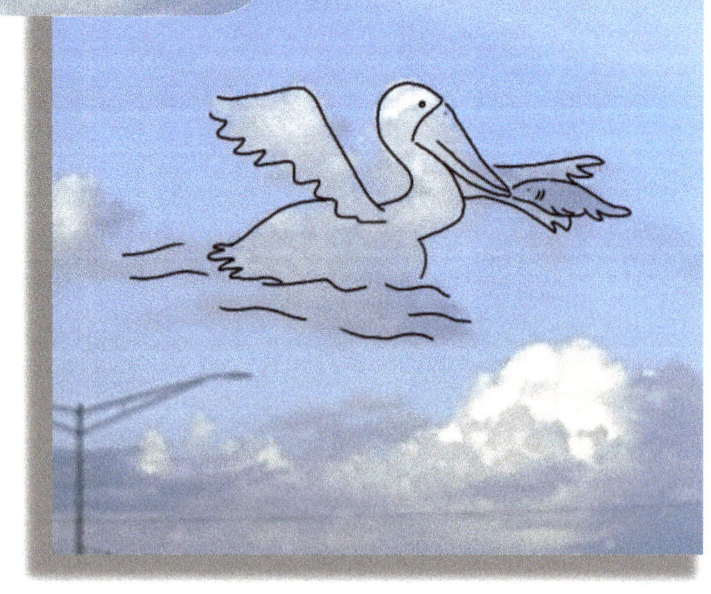

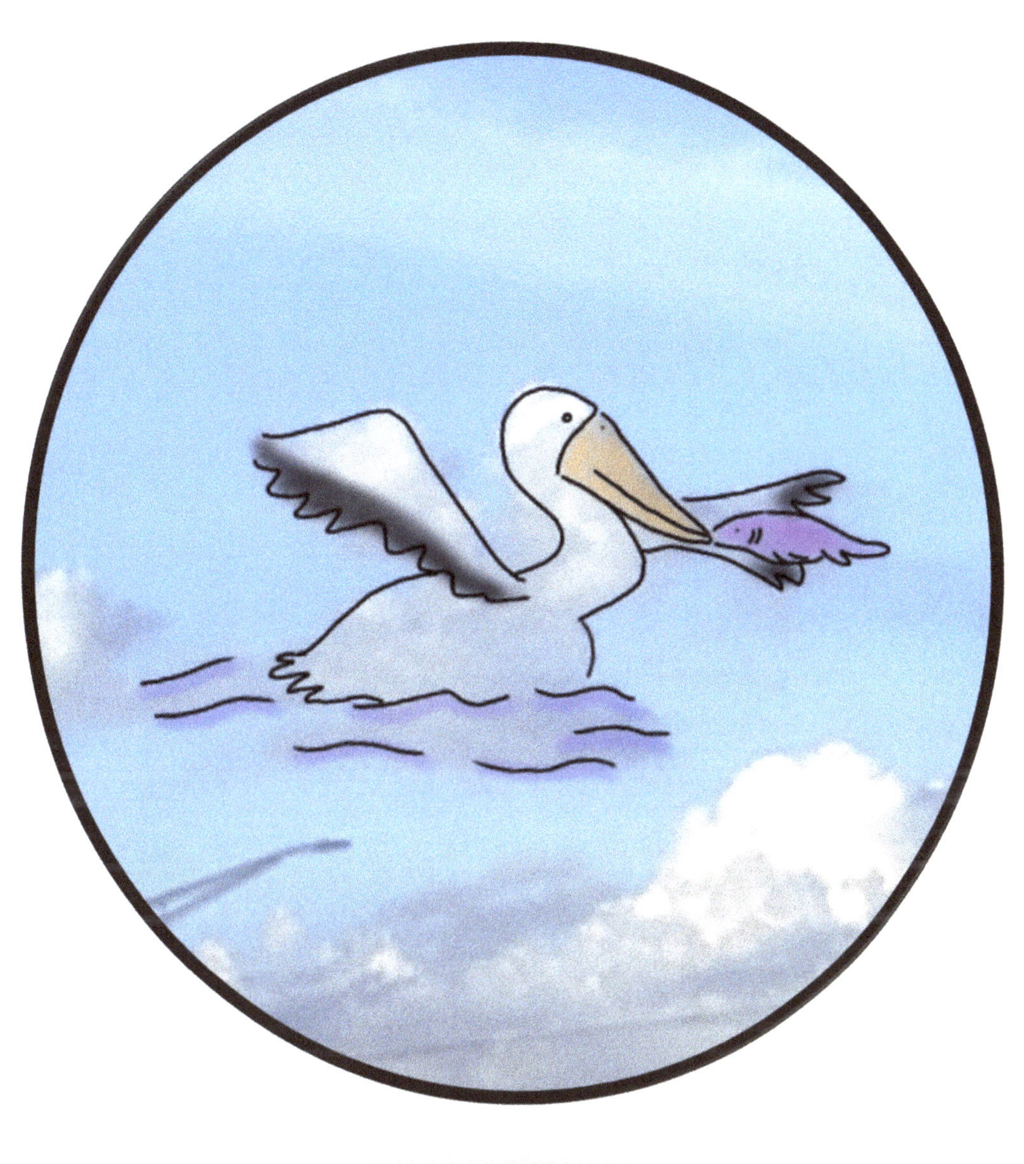

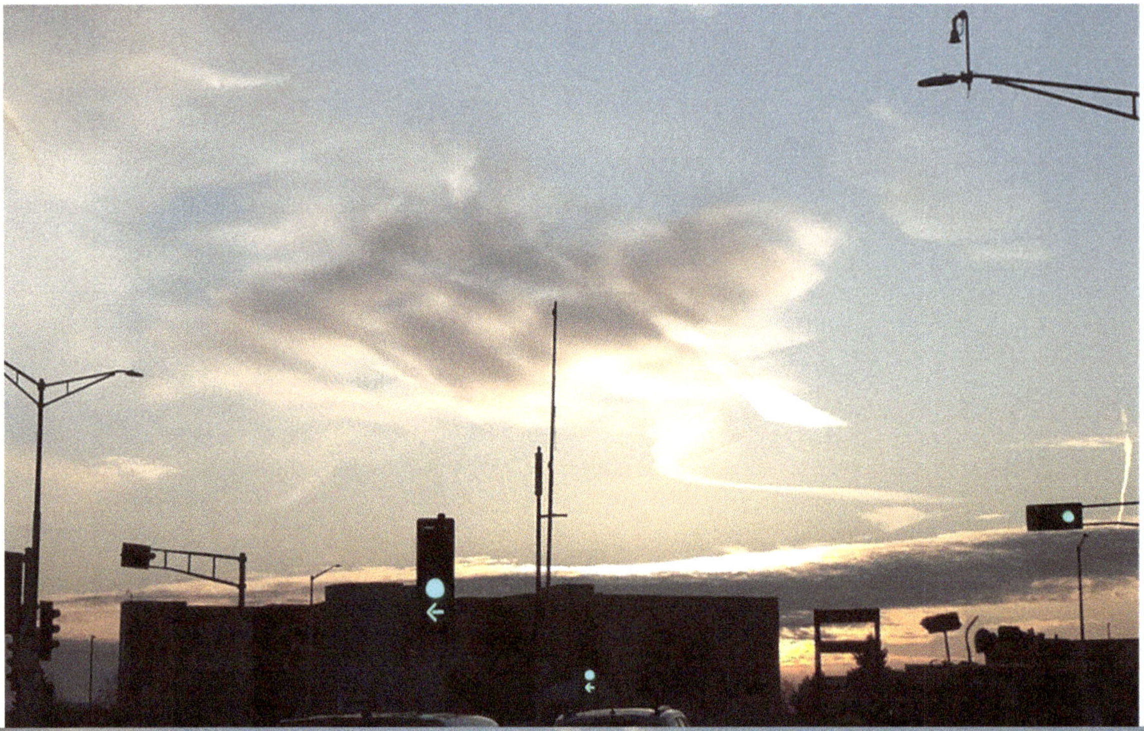

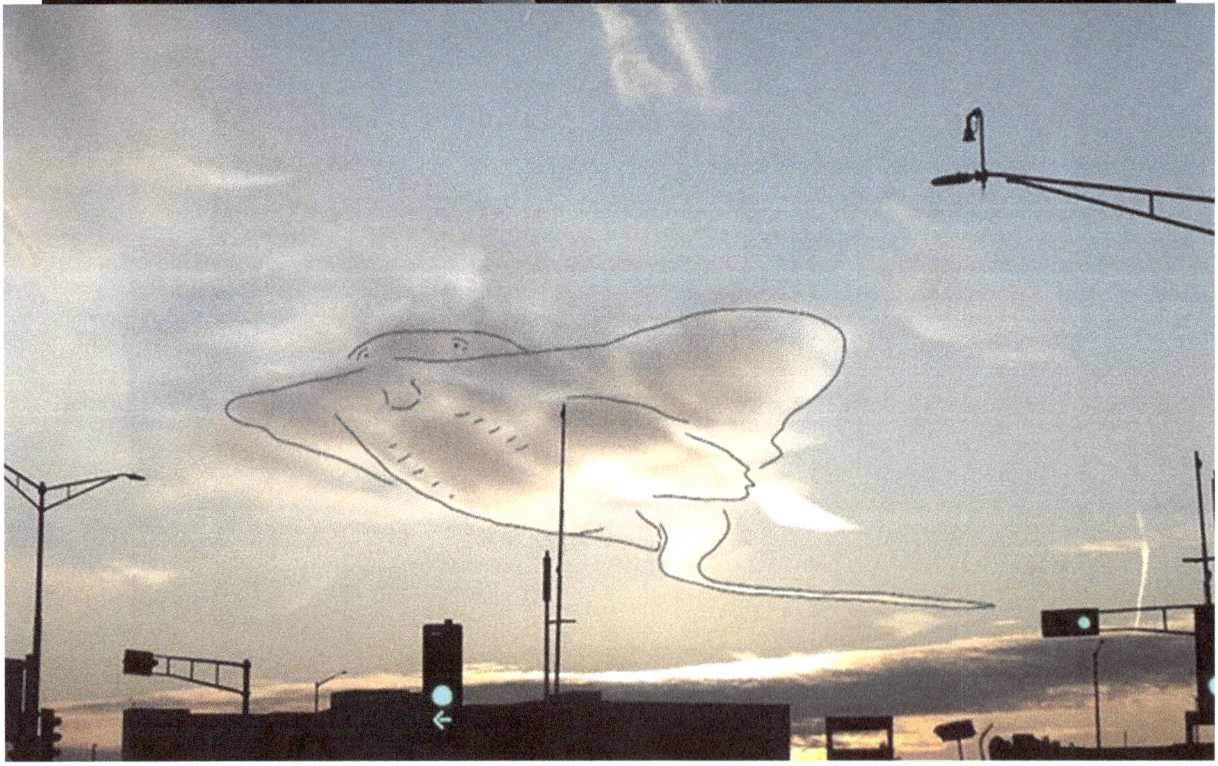

Stingray in the Sky

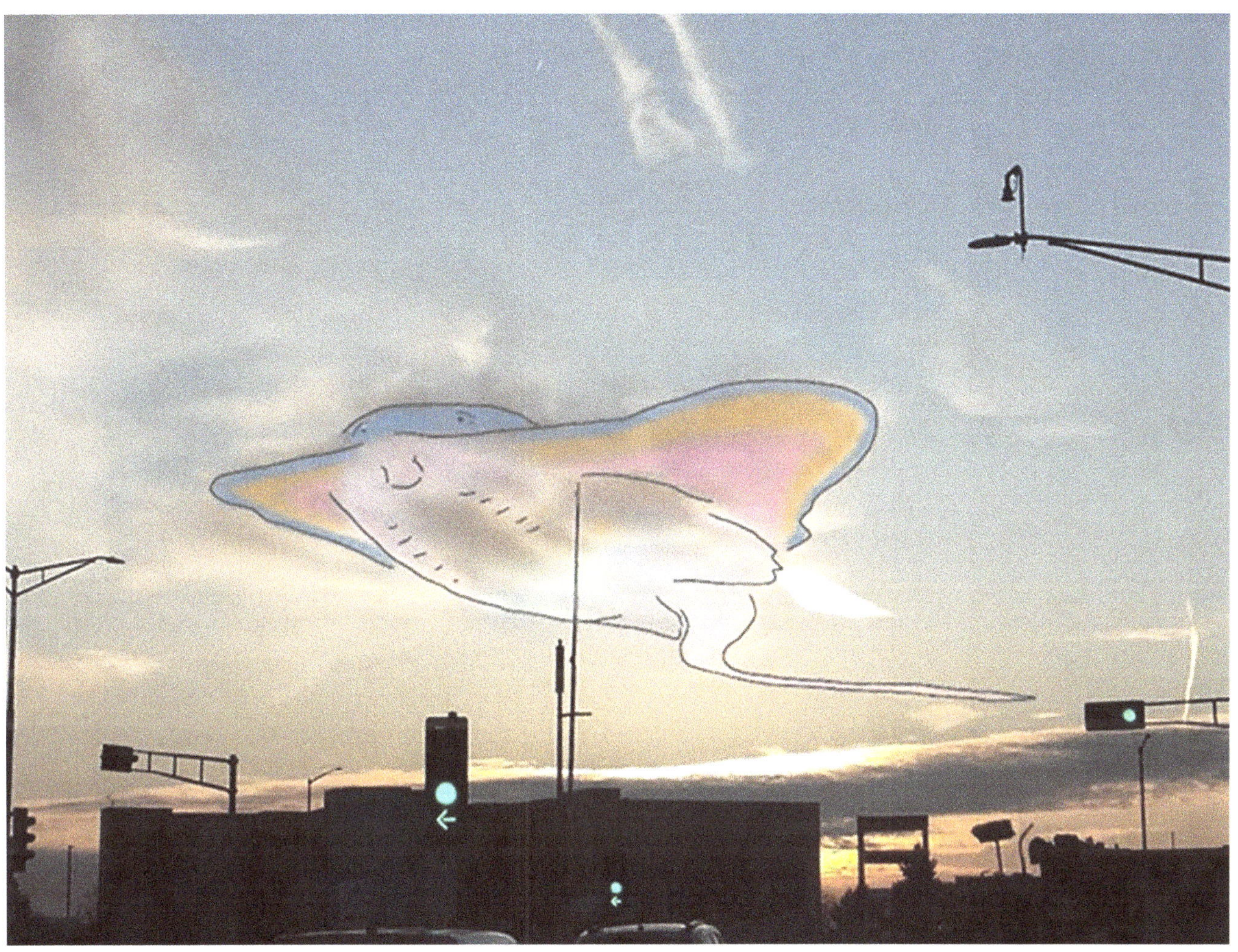

The same friend who sent me the "turtle", which I turned
into a fish, sent me this. We agreed that it was a ray.
(Though he said, "manta ray".)

<u>**Bonus: *Smudge Art***</u>

When I was leaving the breakroom at work, I saw a smudge on a machine. I snapped a picture and when I got home, I drew a bunny.

My daughter saw me drawing, and because of her viewpoint, she said it was a bird.

I turned the picture sideways, and, begrudgingly, drew a bird.
(*don't tell her, but I think the bird is cuter*)

So...

Bunny or Bird?

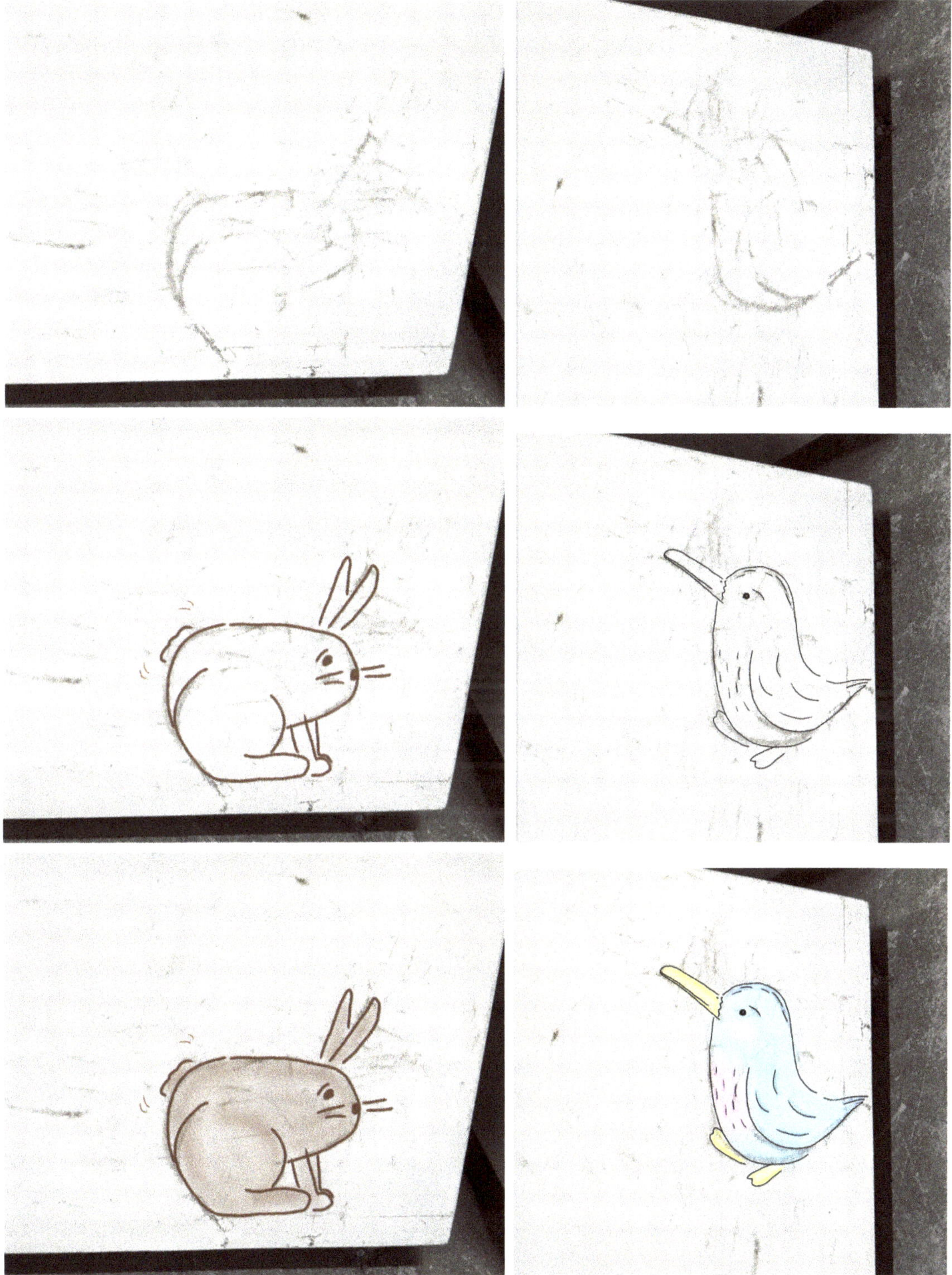

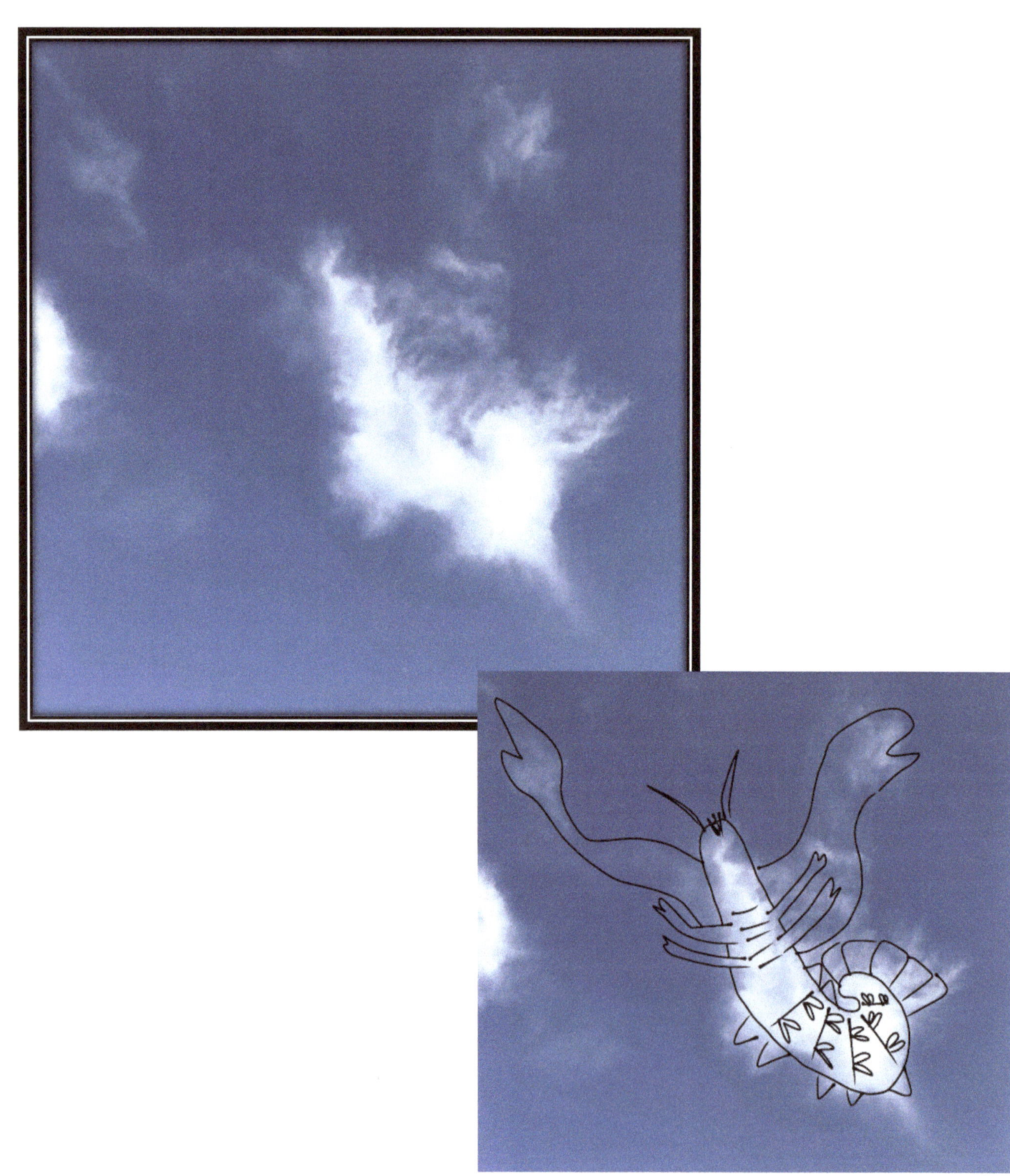

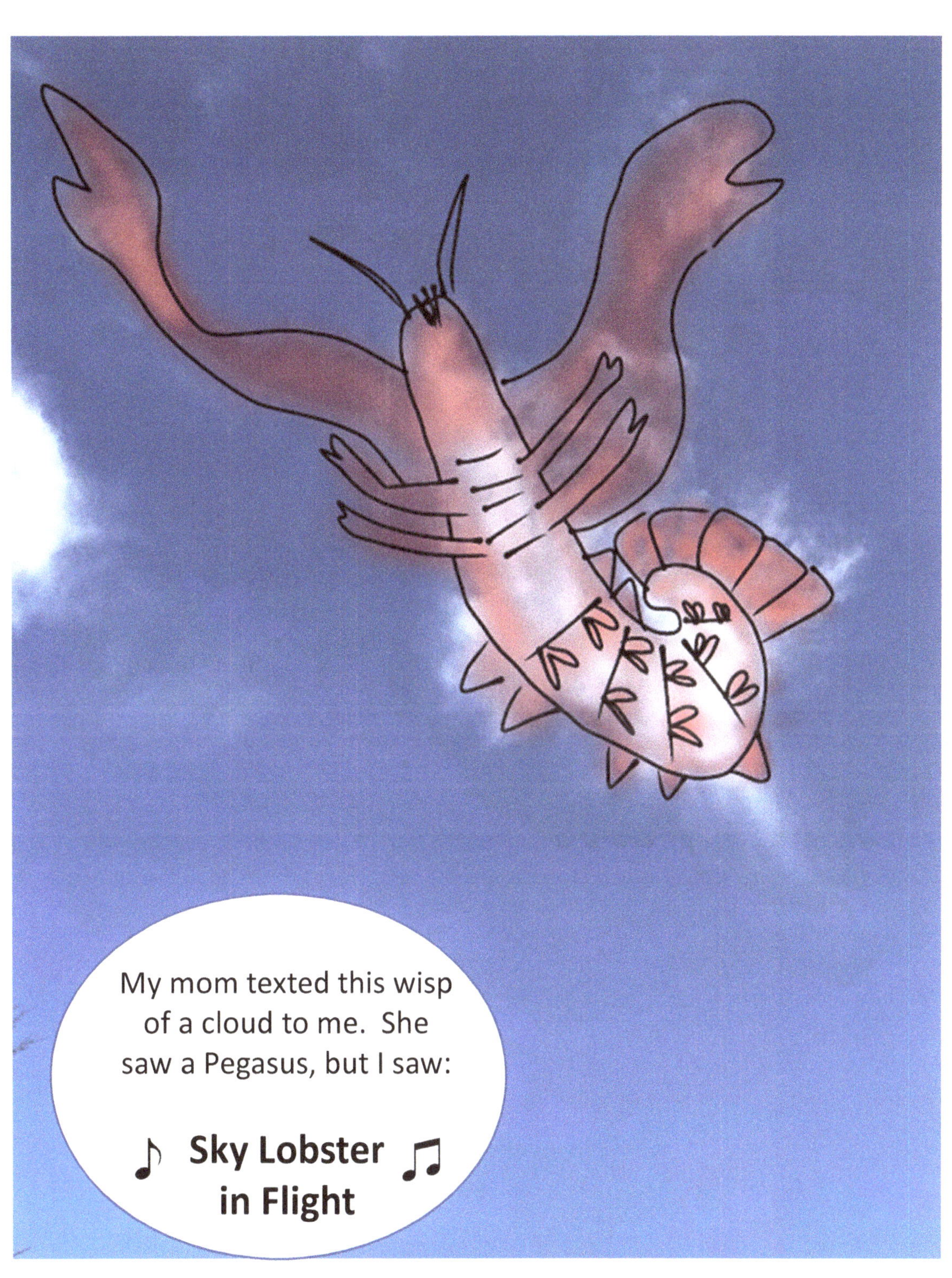

My mom texted this wisp of a cloud to me. She saw a Pegasus, but I saw:
♪ Sky Lobster ♫ in Flight

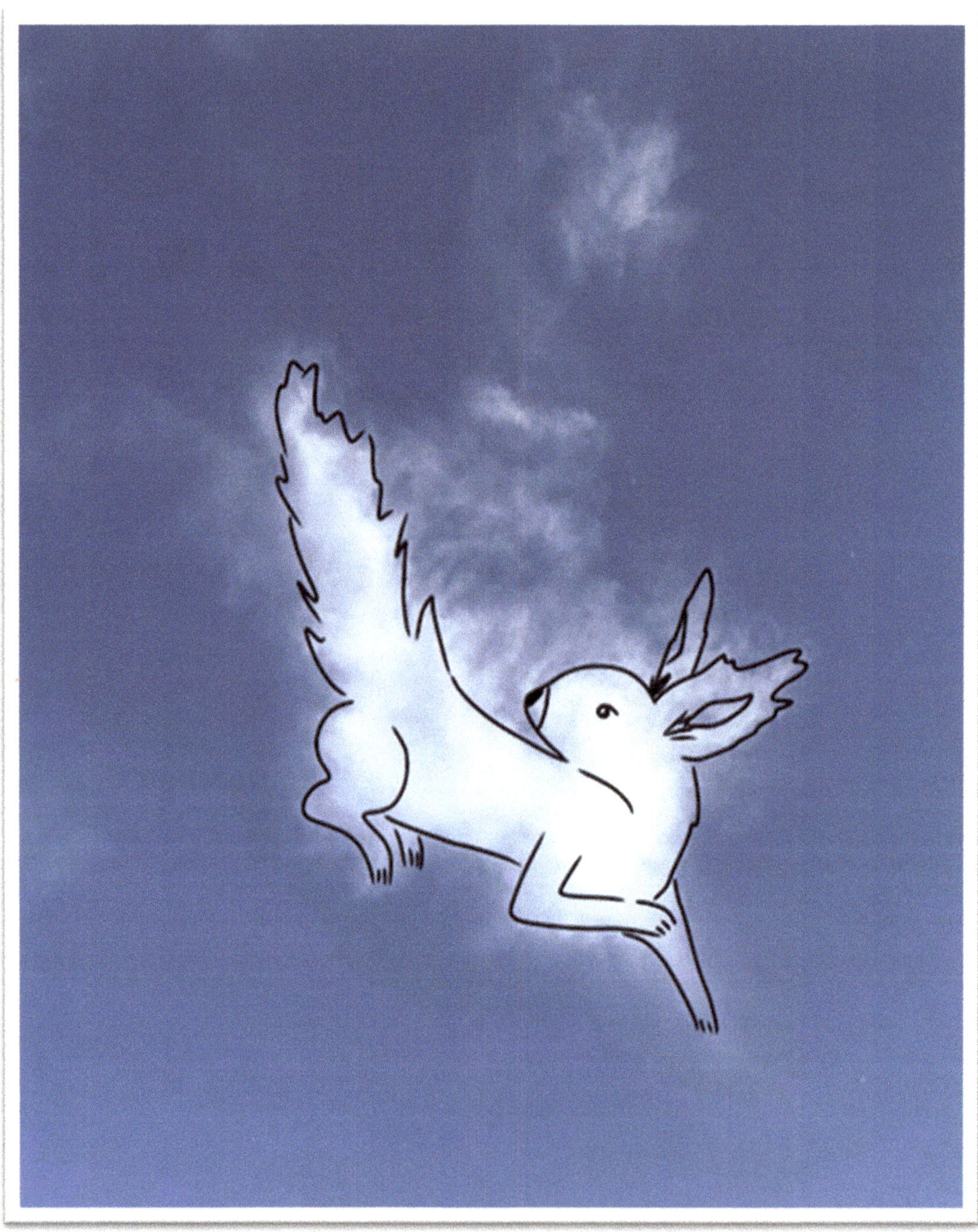

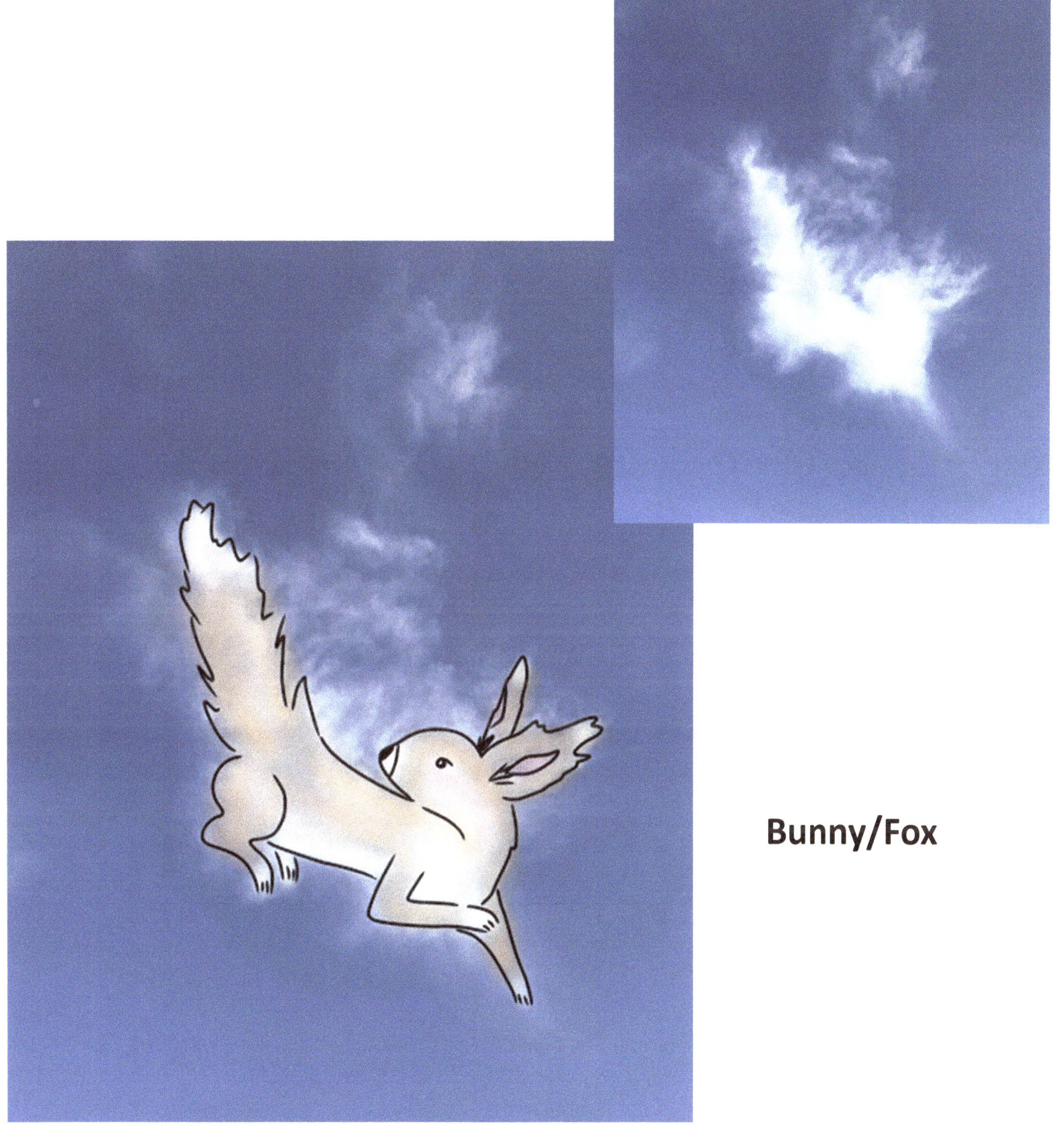
Bunny/Fox

I have a few clouds that I've reused
for other pictures.

It's amazing how the same shape can
be seen in different ways, even by
the same person.

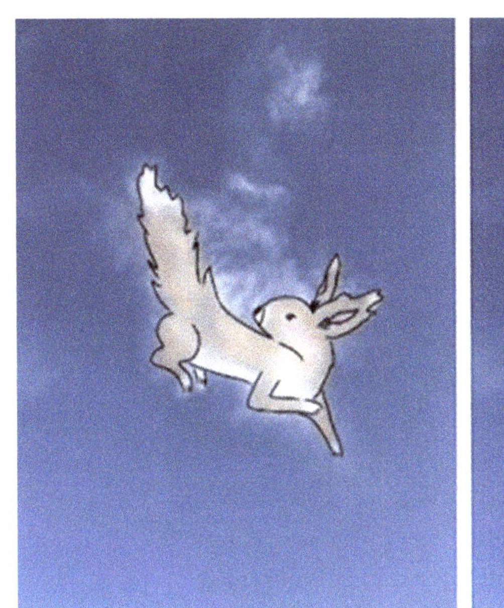
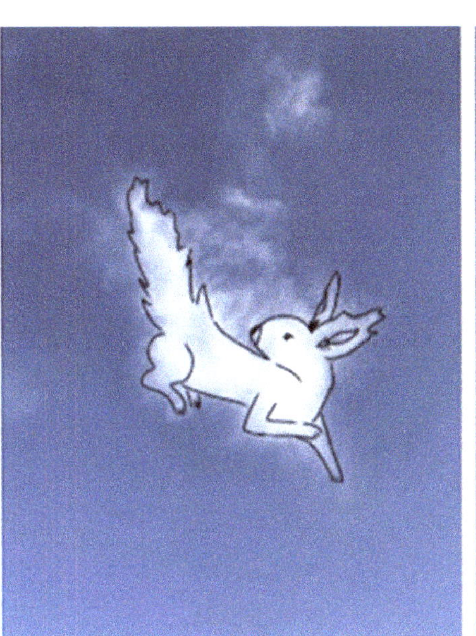
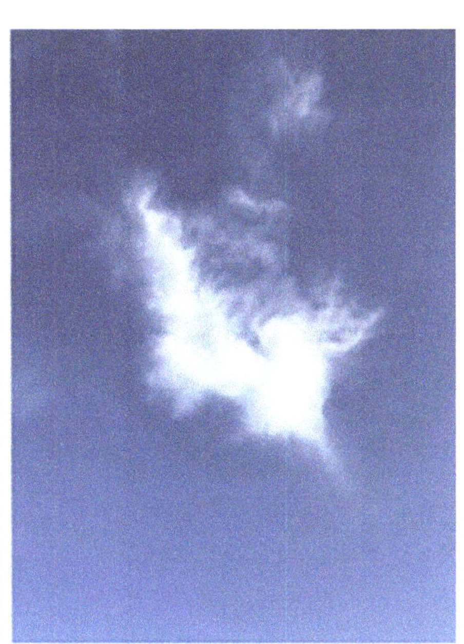
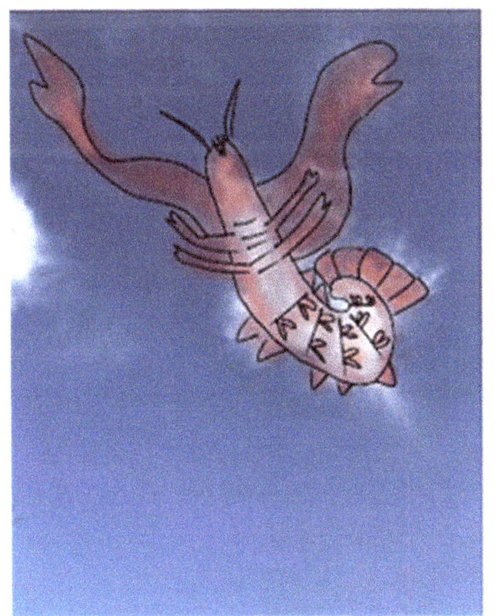
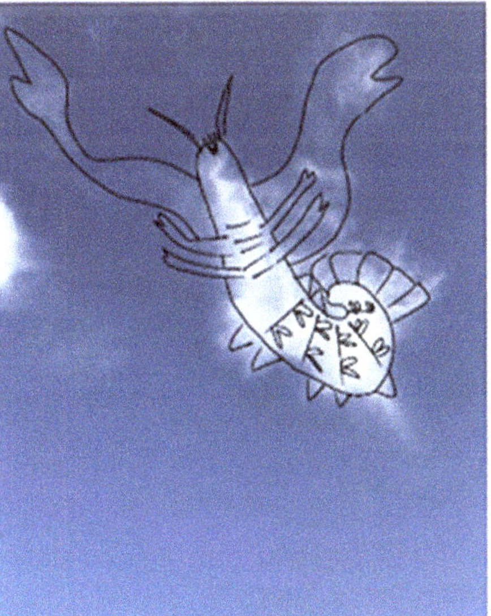
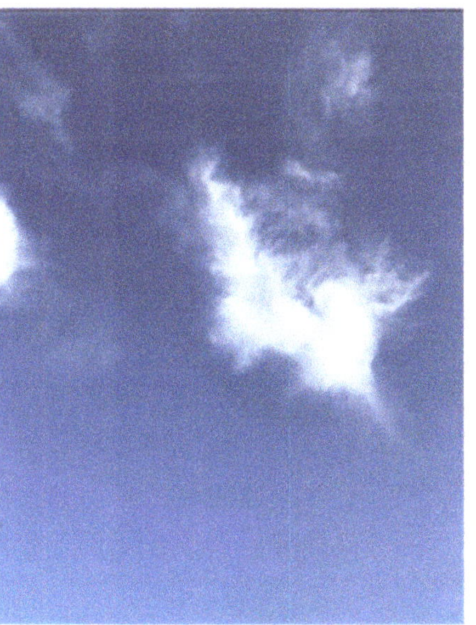

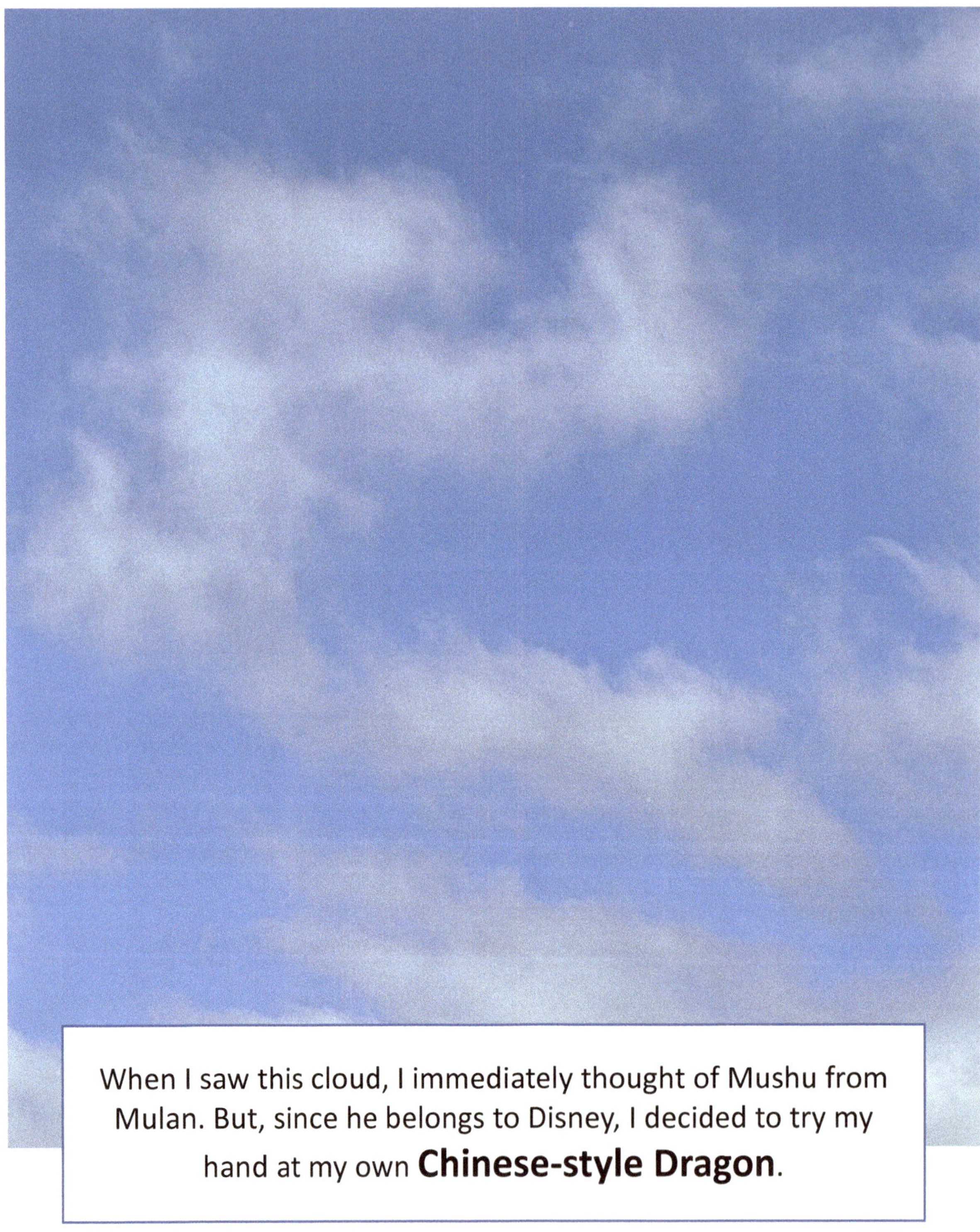

When I saw this cloud, I immediately thought of Mushu from Mulan. But, since he belongs to Disney, I decided to try my hand at my own **Chinese-style Dragon**.

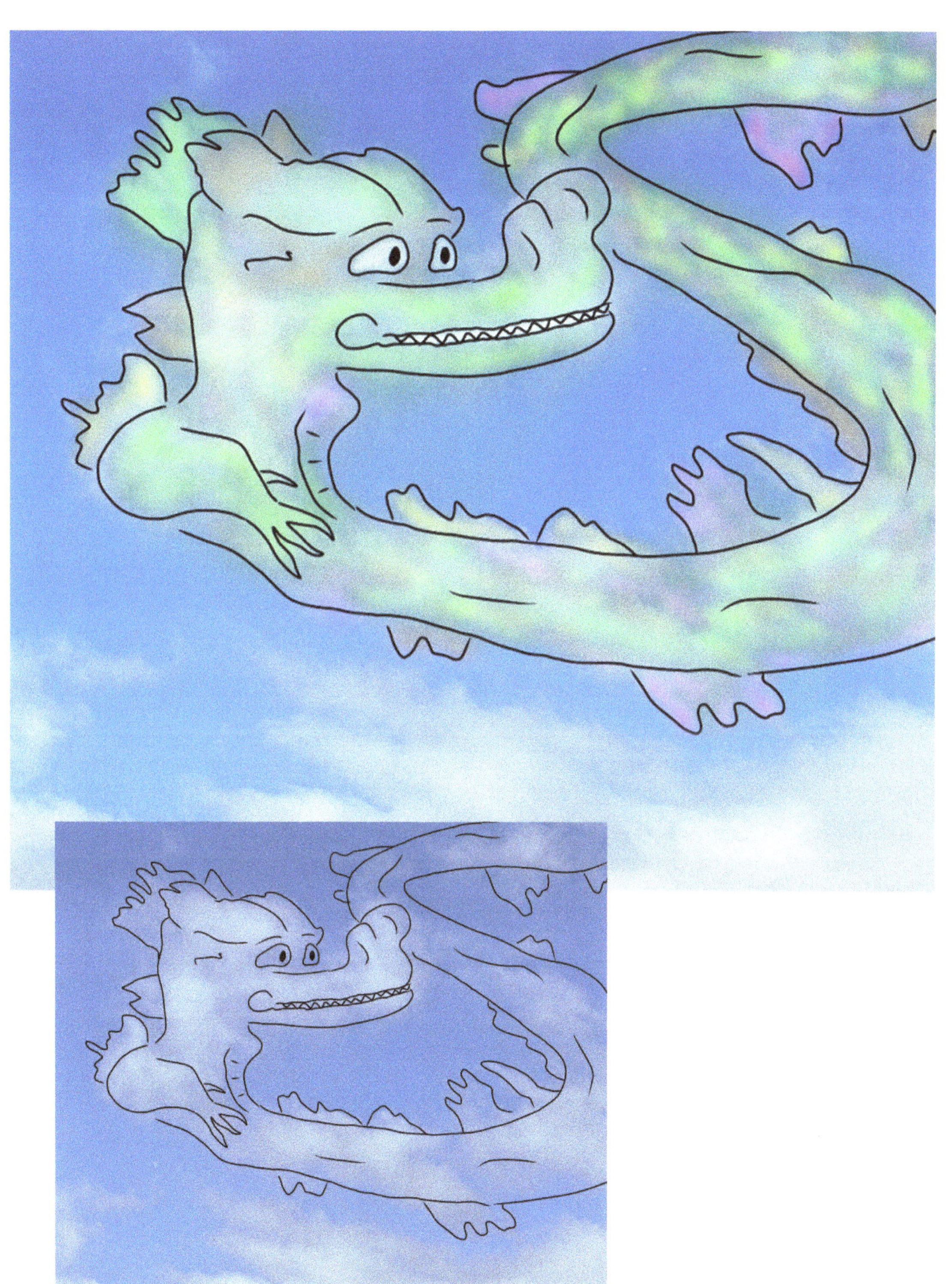

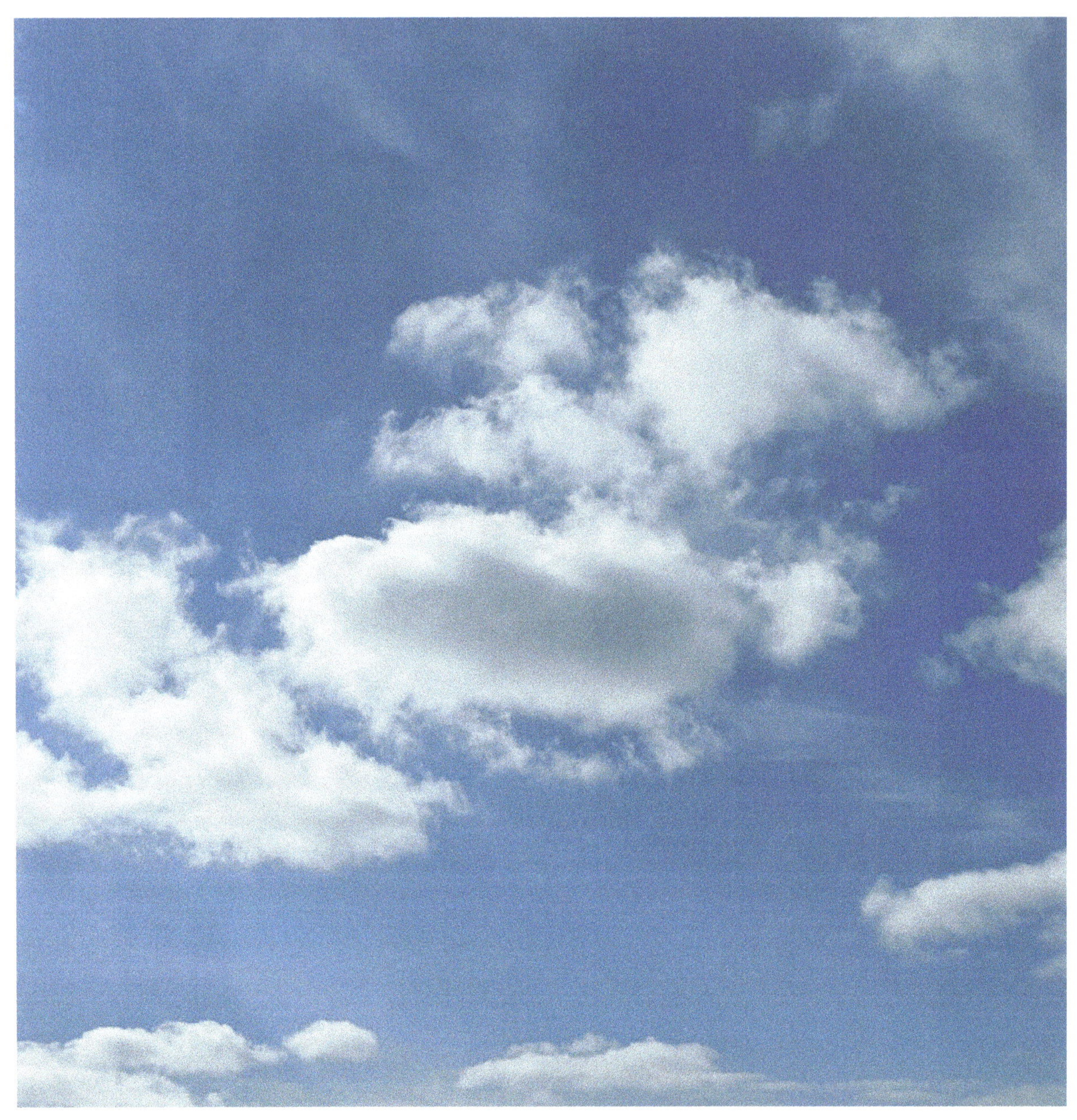

Ghost on a Rocking Horse

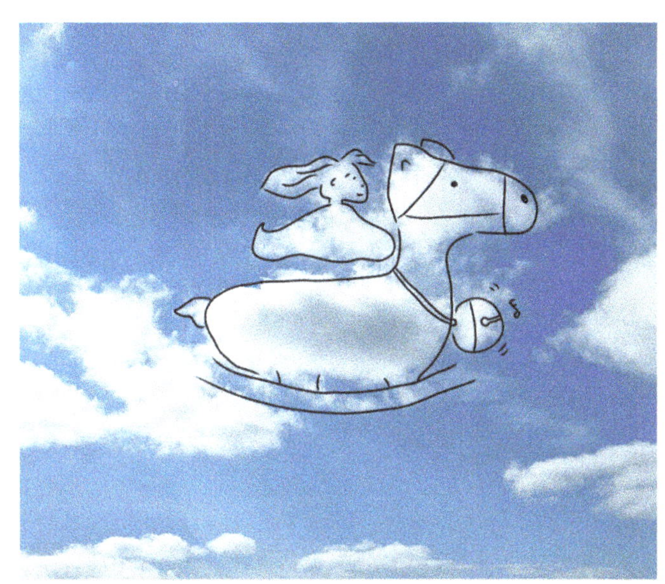

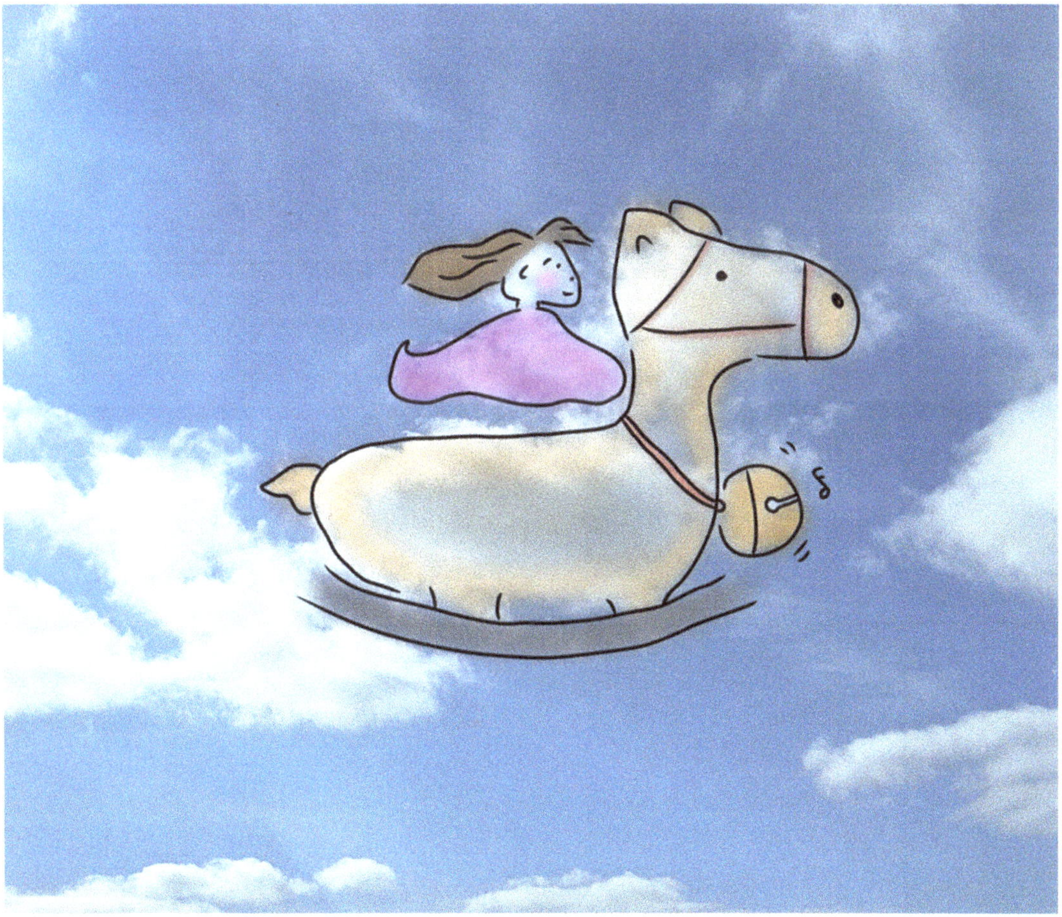

I envisioned a screeching raptor with a crown on its head.
However, my hand drew a giant parrot instead.
After a quick redraw, I got...

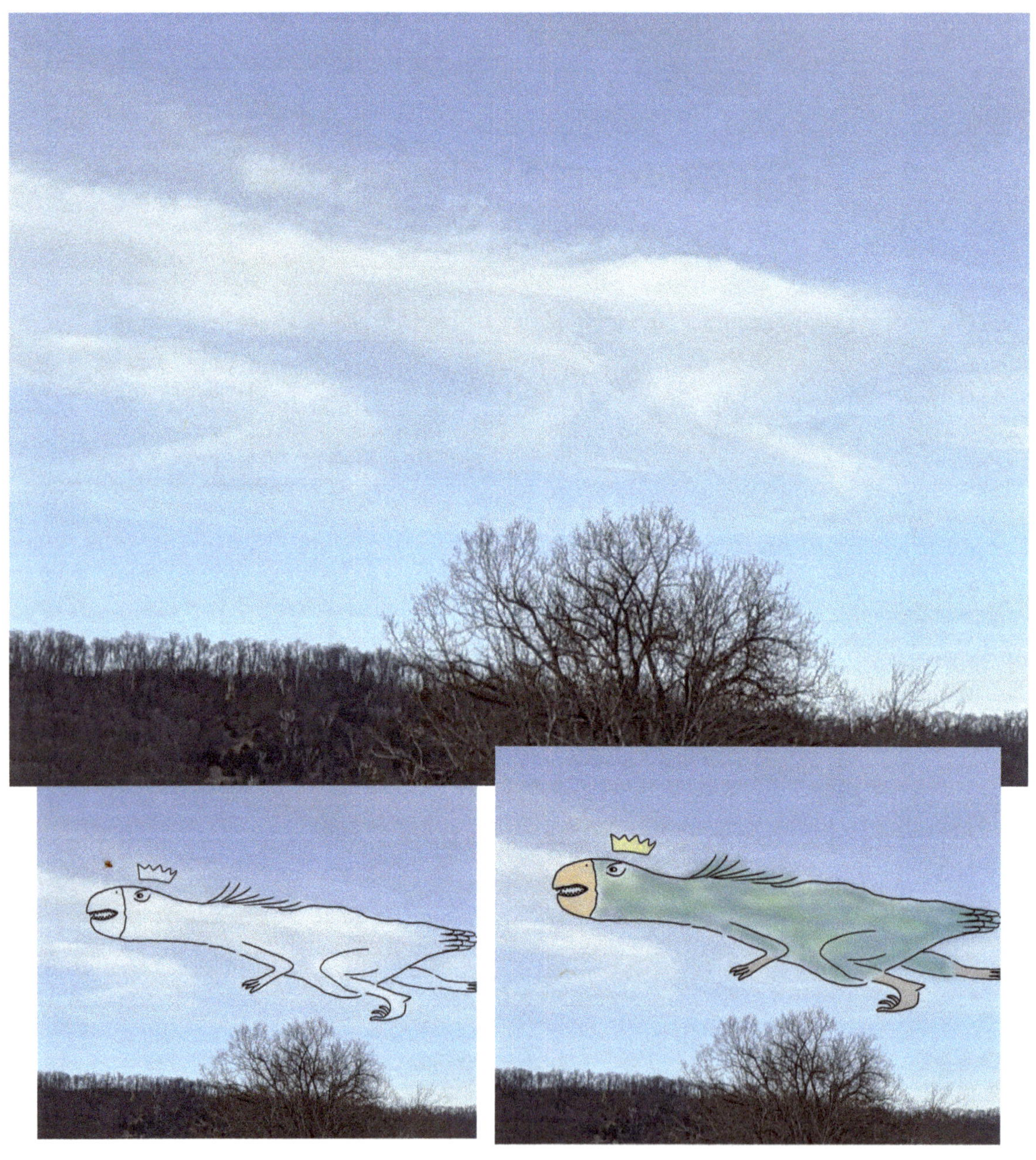

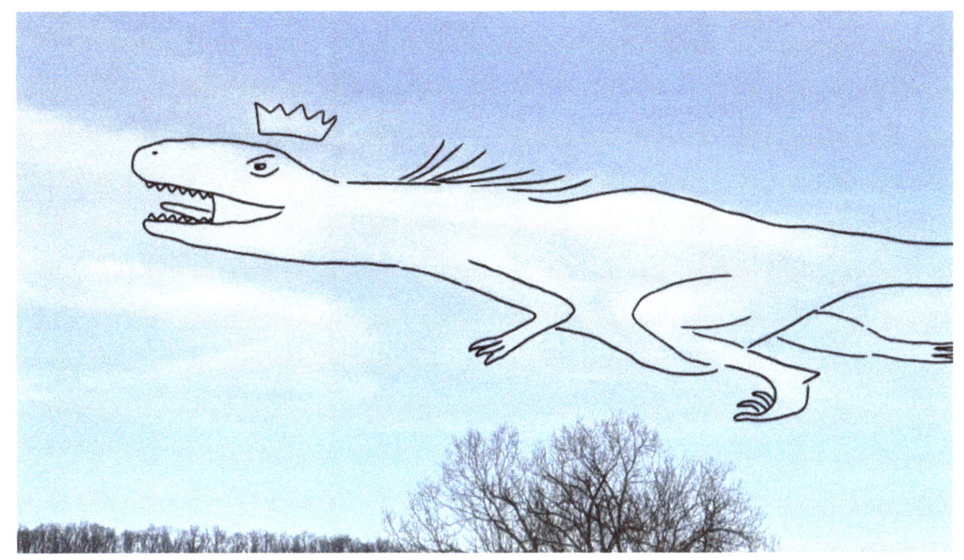

Dino King

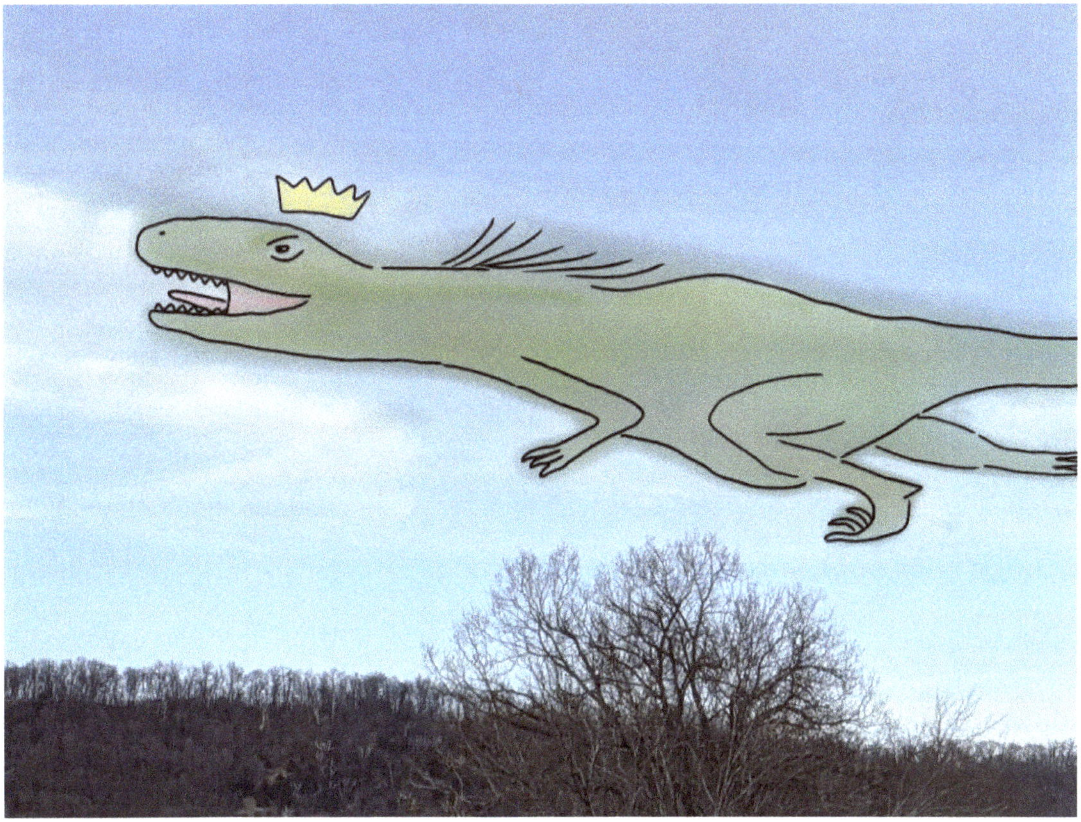

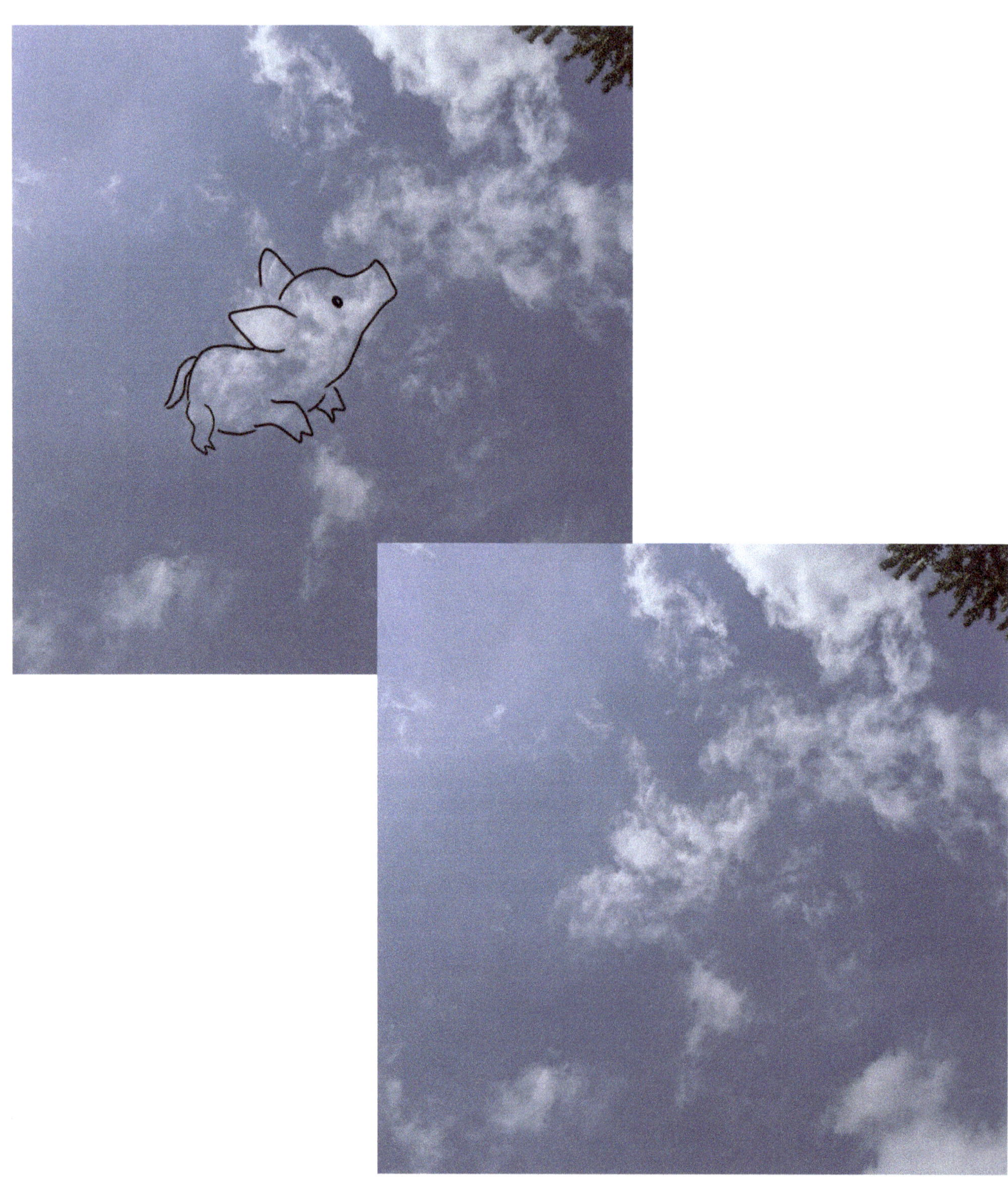

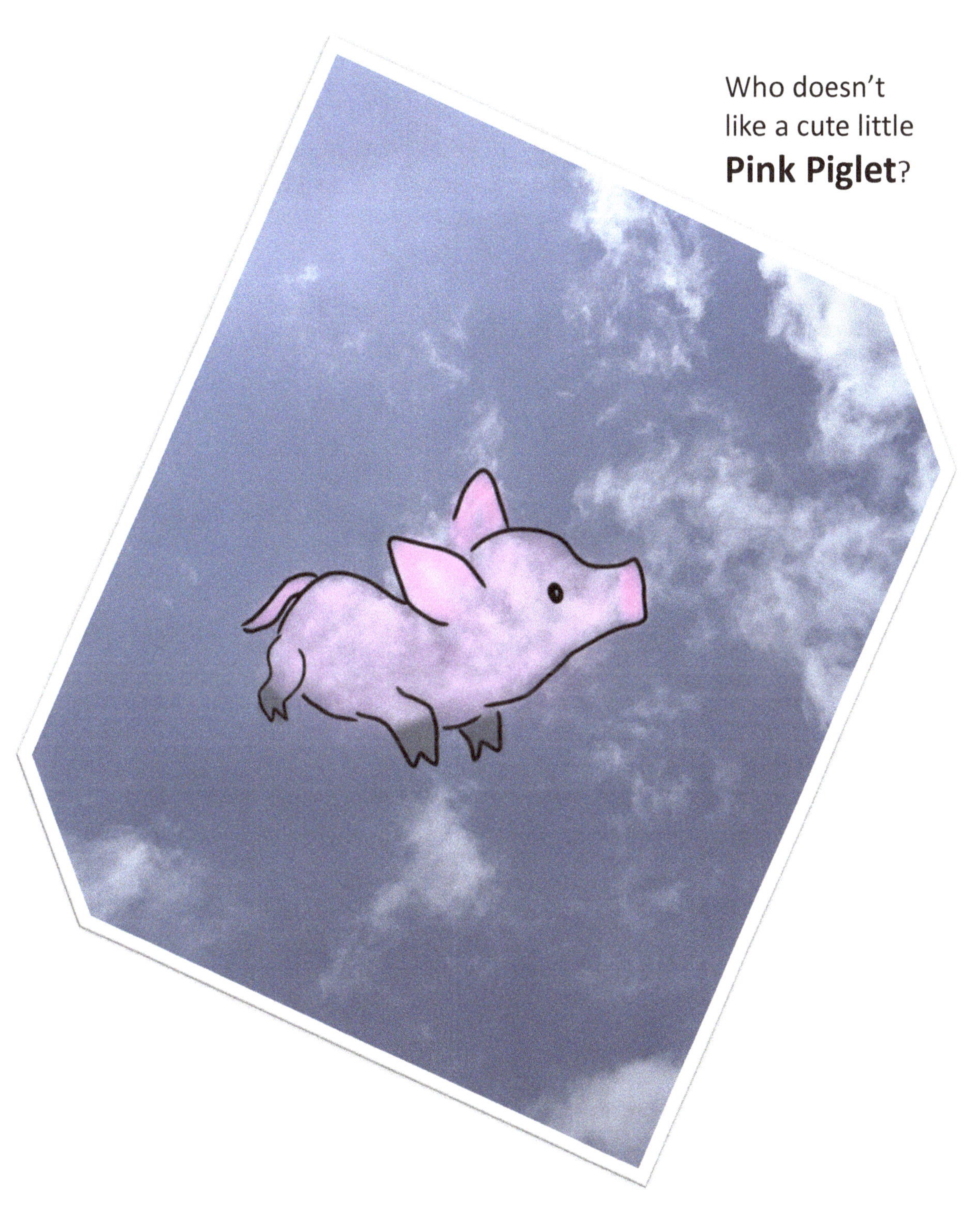

Who doesn't
like a cute little
Pink Piglet?

A friend, and fellow writer, snapped this picture and suggested
it was a snail, so a snail I drew. ☺
He also suggested that it might make a good poem, and as an
over-achiever, I wrote one.

"Little" Snail

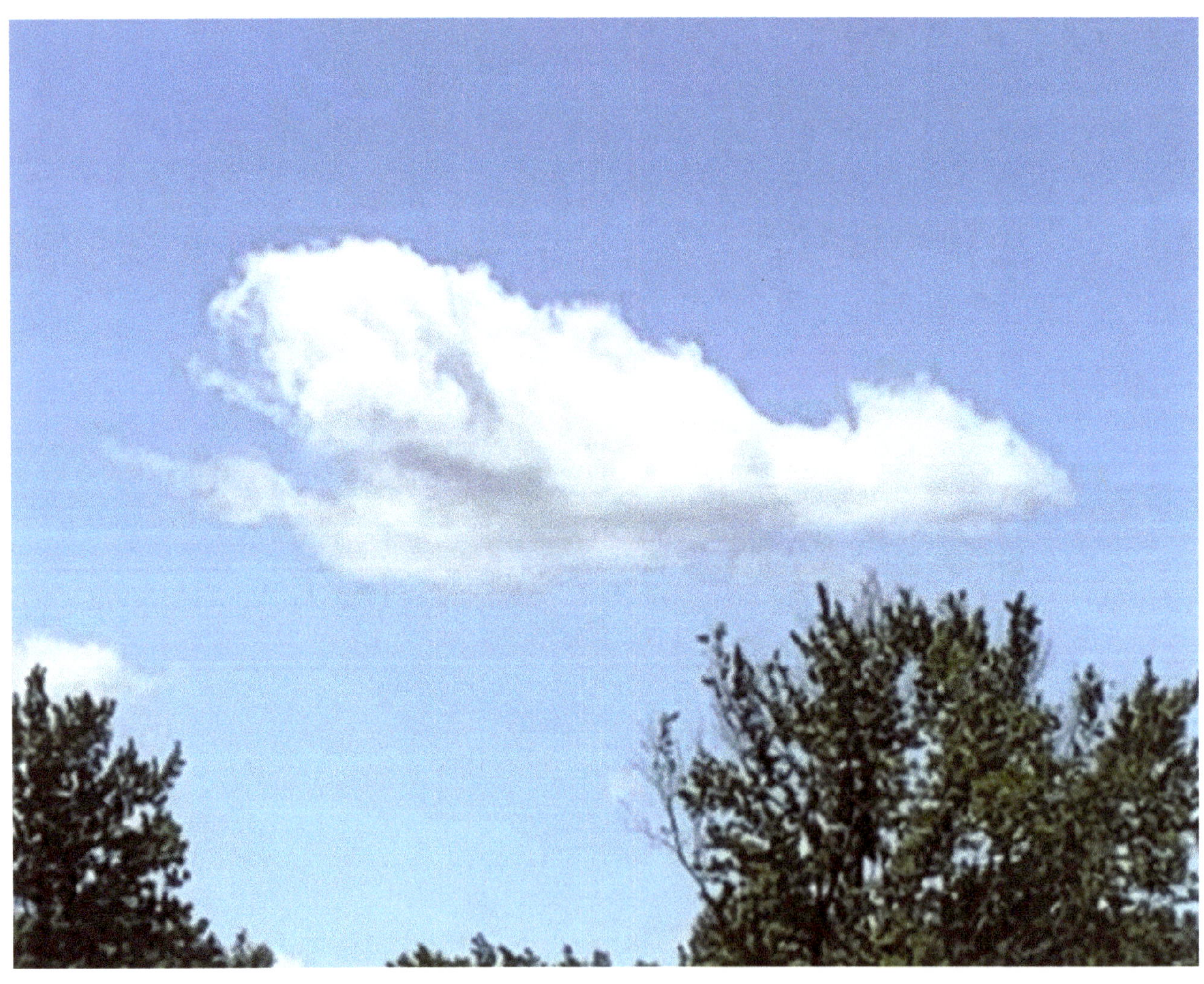

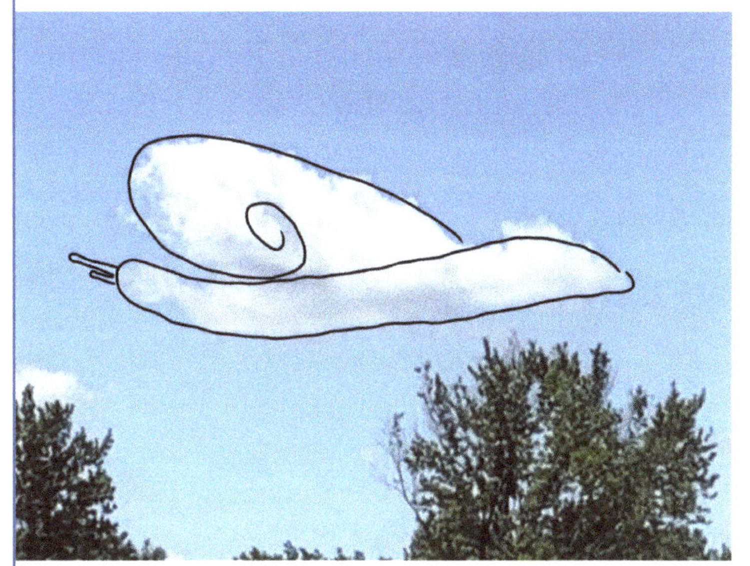

A wispy creature
Floating by
Sliding on a current

A slimy trail
Left behind
A traveled path; transparent

With a roving foot
It moves about
A large shell on its back

The stalk-like eyes
Searching for
The rest of its snail pack

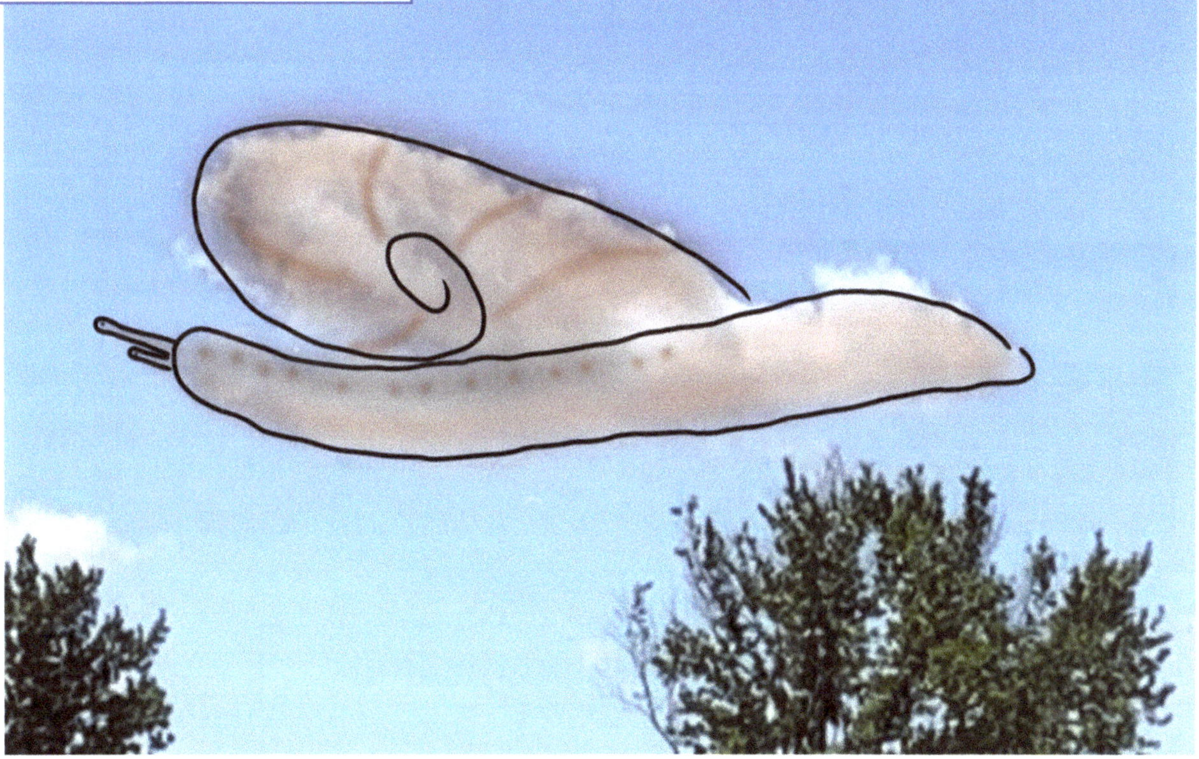

Like several other pictures in this book, while I was
working on the snail, I started to see something else...

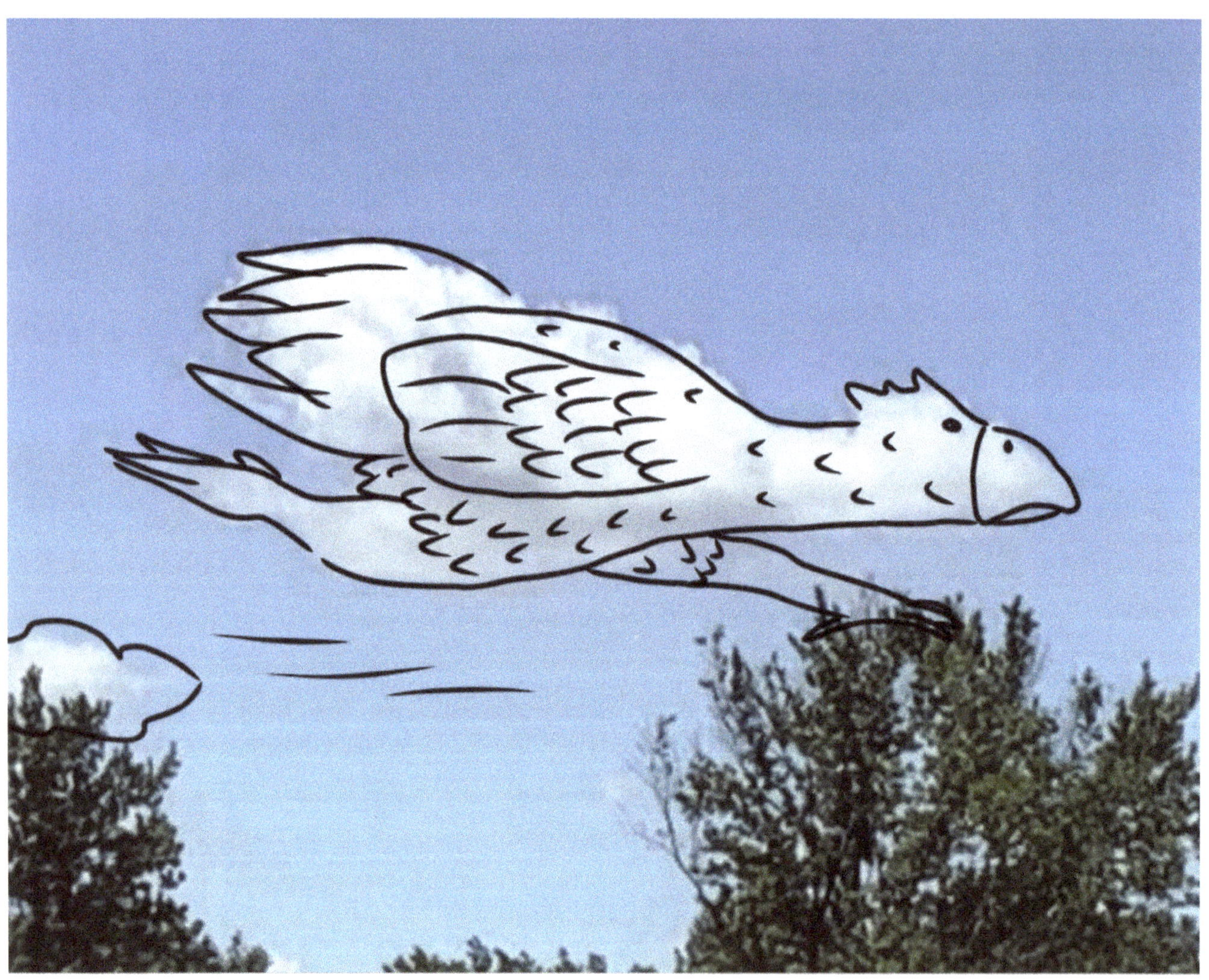

Chicken on the Run

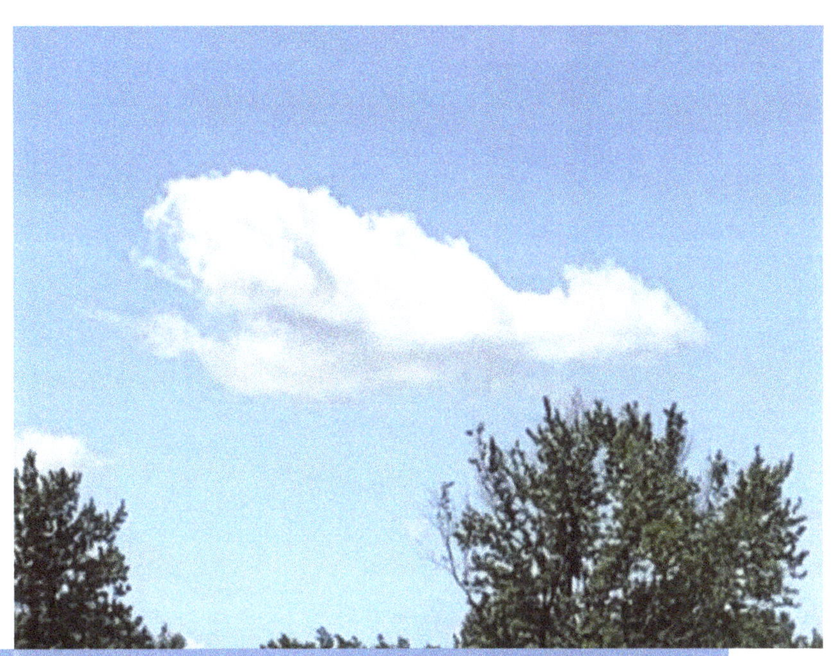

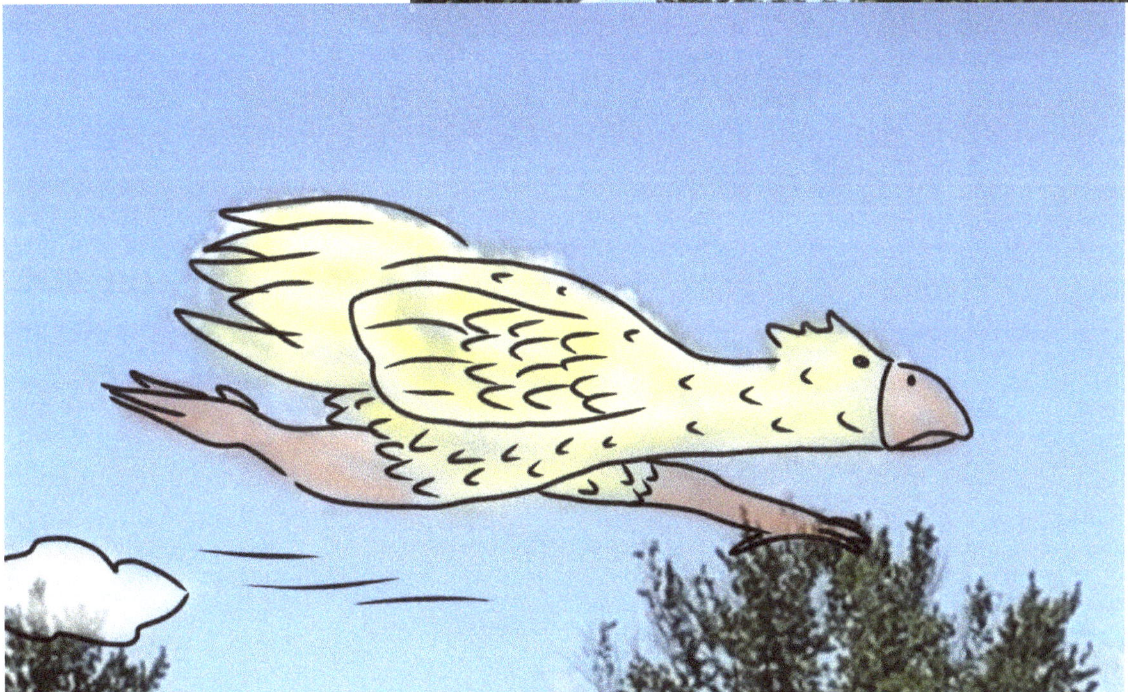

Not every drawing has to be elaborate. There's nothing wrong with seeing something simple in the clouds.

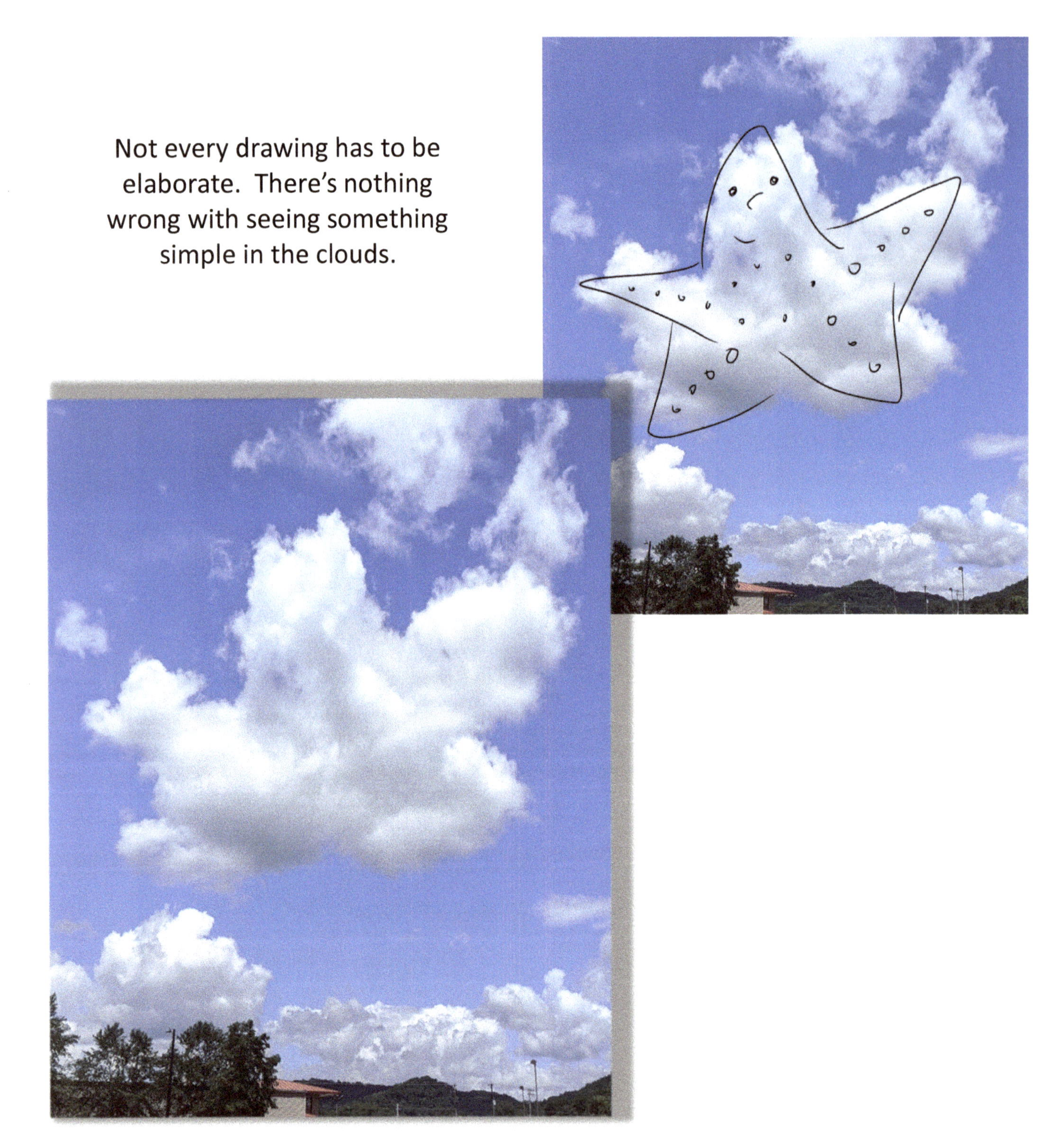

Starfish

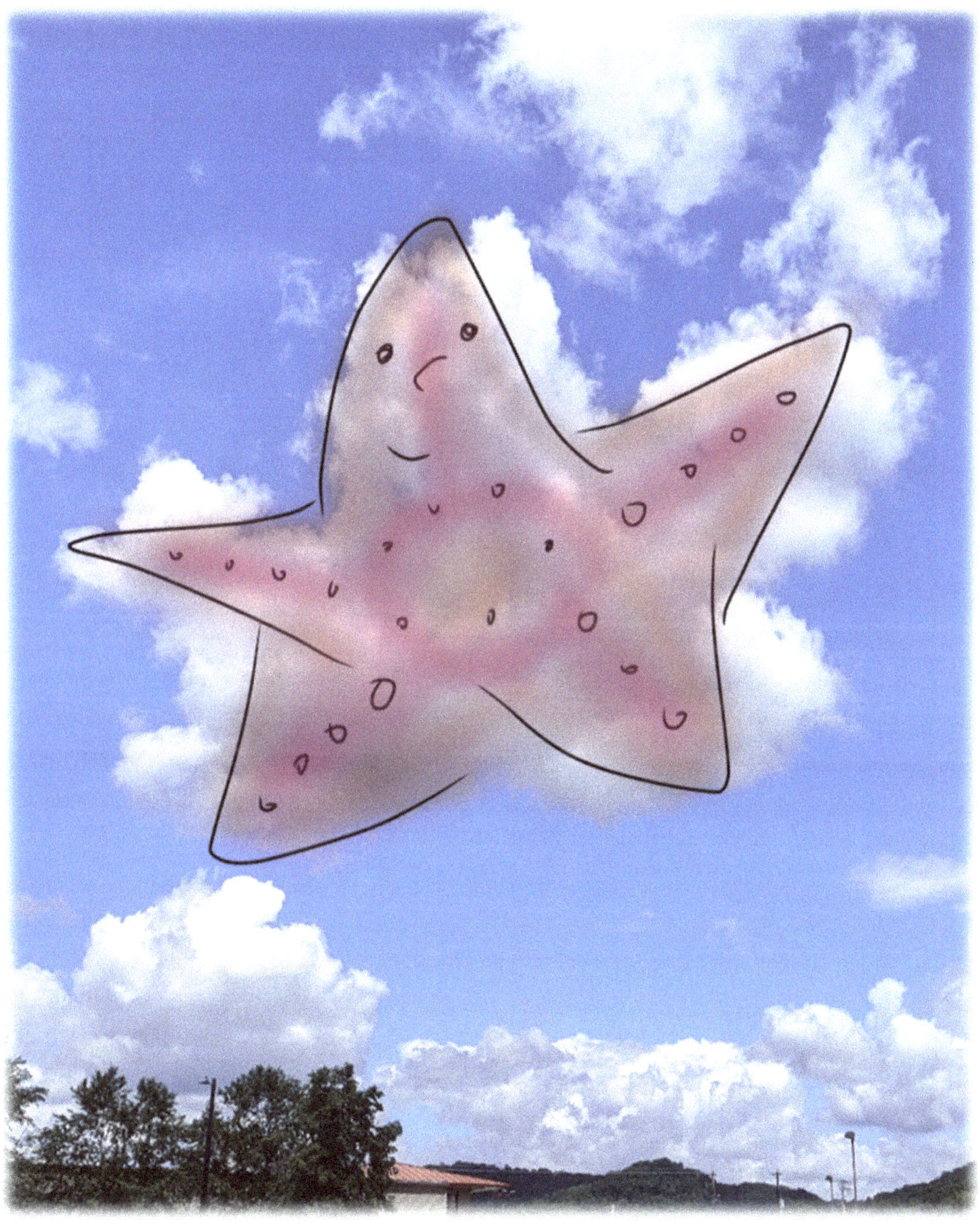

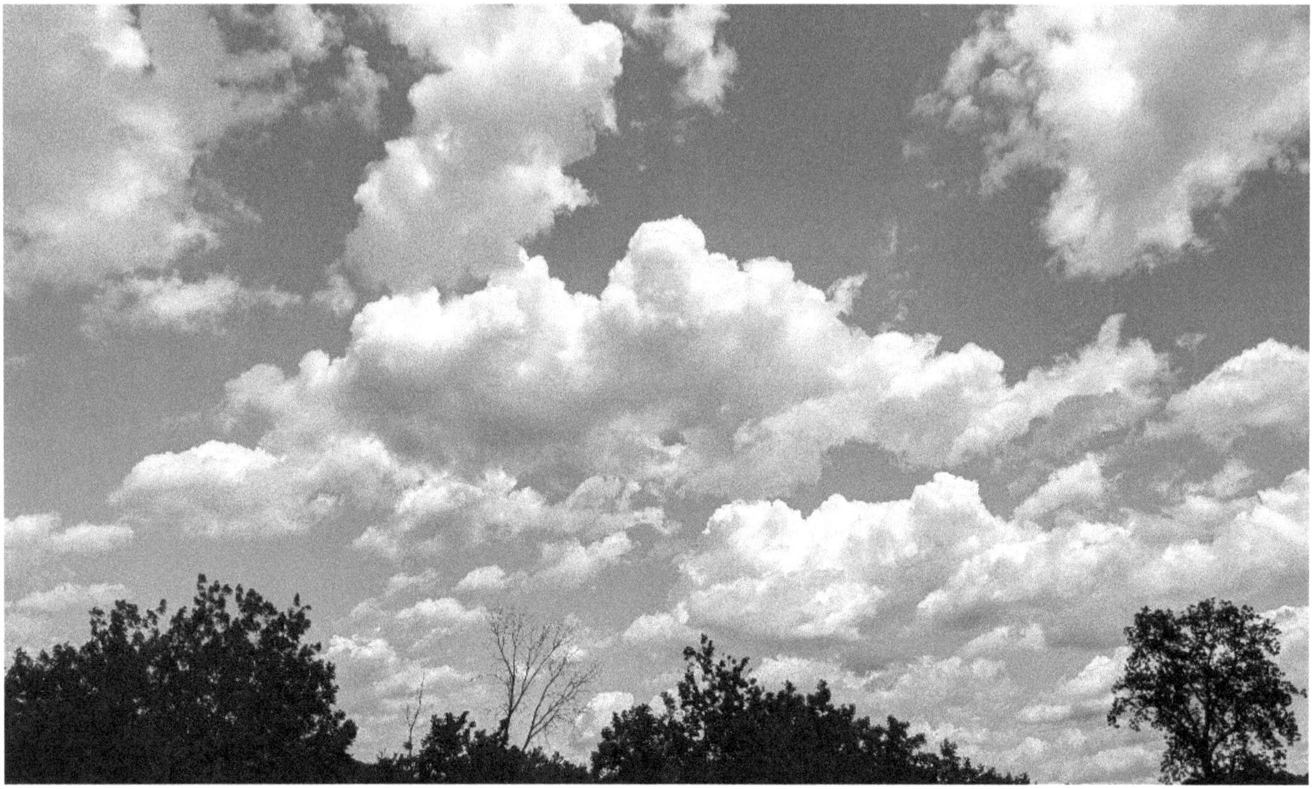

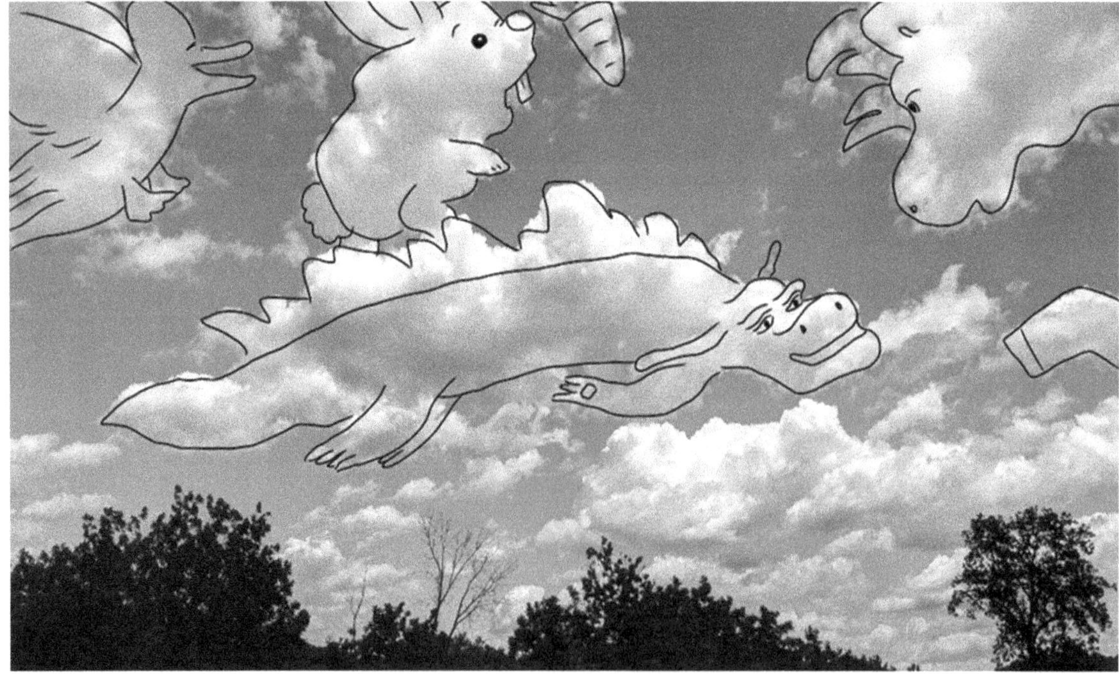

Sometimes, though, I get carried away drawing on clouds.
This last one I call: **Chaos in the Sky**

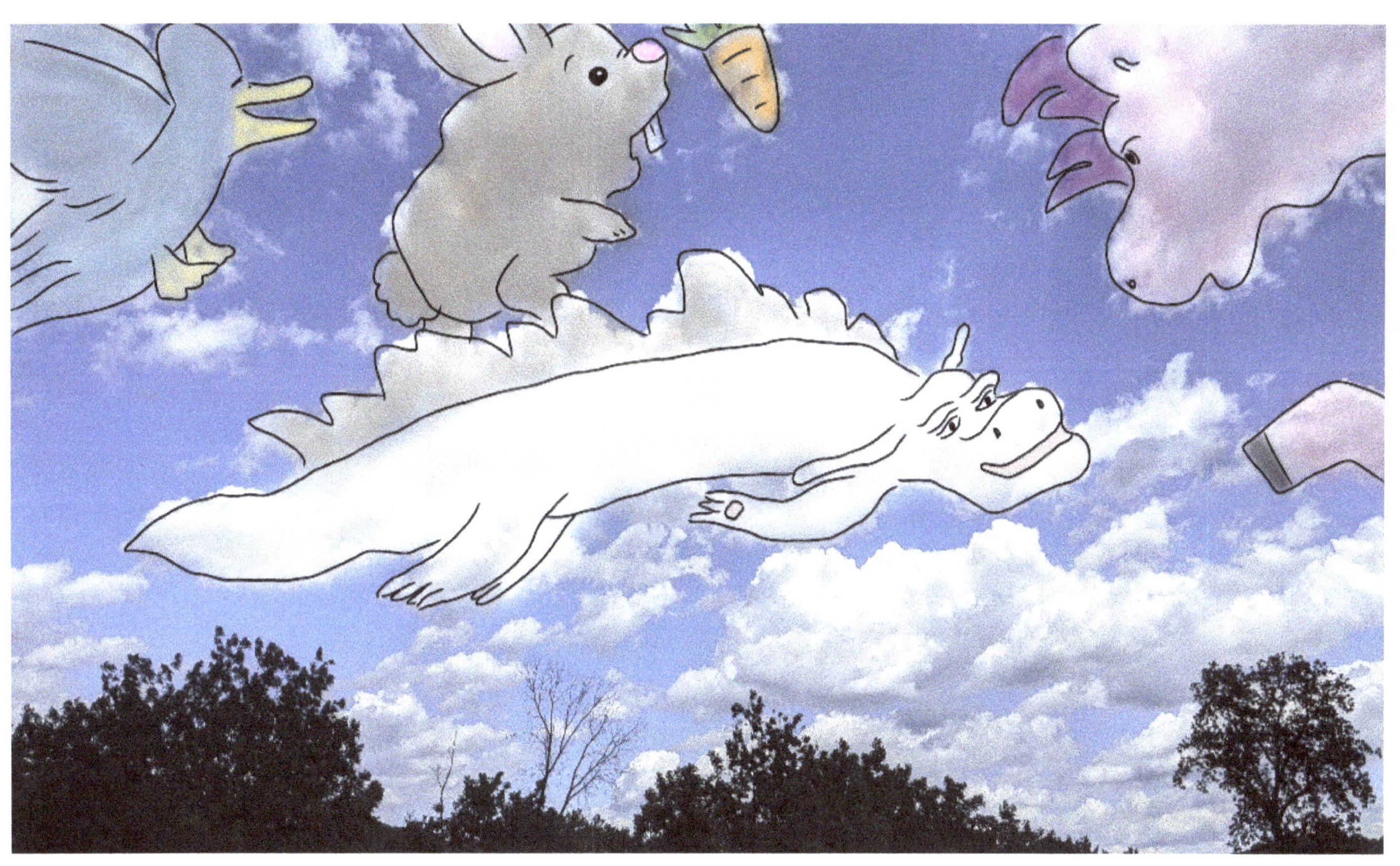

My daughter's drawing using "Angry Fish"

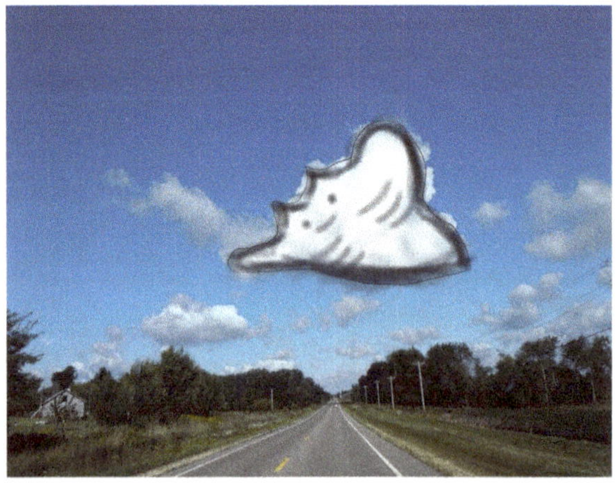

<u>**About the Author:**</u>

Nicki Snyder currently lives in Wisconsin with her family, and a menagerie of pets. And while she dislikes the cold, she loves the beauty of the area, and the warmth of the people that she's met there.

Nicki has been writing since she was a young teen. Her first book, *The Circus Elephant*, was published when she was 19, and was written in middle school as a class project.

Since joining a local writing group, her passion for writing and publishing has grown. She now has several books in the works.

#cloudart was a fun book for Nicki to do. It combines her love of writing and illustrating. She already has a file full of new pictures, and hopes to have a sequel to *#cloudart* within the next year or two.

If you'd like to check out more artwork by Nicki Snyder, she is under **cannibalbananas** on several social media platforms.